The Smarter Bet™ Guide to Slots and Video Poker

Basil Nestor

STERLING PUBLISHING CO., INC.
NEW YORK

For Freddy and Jenny.

Play your best game every day,
and the winning will take care of itself.

Library of Congress Cataloging-in-Publication Data Available

10 9 8 7 6 5 4 3 2 1

A Primrose Production
Design by Lynne Yeamans

Published by Sterling Publishing Co., Inc.
387 Park Avenue South, New York, NY 10016
Previously published by Dorset Press
Copyright © 2002 by Basil Nestor
Distributed in Canada by Sterling Publishing
℅ Canadian Manda Group, One Atlantic Avenue, Suite 105
Toronto, Ontario, Canada M6K 3E7
Distributed in Great Britain by Chrysalis Books Group PLC
The Chrysalis Building, Bramley Road, London W10 6SP, England
Distributed in Australia by Capricorn Link (Australia) Pty. Ltd.
P.O. Box 704, Windsor, NSW 2756, Australia

Printed in Hong Kong
All rights reserved

Sterling ISBN 1-4027-1563-3

This book contains the opinions and ideas of its author, and it is designed to provide
useful advice to the reader on the subject covered. The publisher and the author
specifically disclaim any responsibility for any liability, loss, or risk (financial, personal, or otherwise) that may be claimed or incurred as a consequence, directly or
indirectly, of the use and/or application of the contents of this book.

Contents

Introduction

The Reel History of Slots

ONE HUNDRED FIFTY YEARS AGO, gambling in North America was dominated by cards, dice, wheels, and lotteries. Faro was the most popular card game, but poker was a fashionable newcomer and it was gaining ground. This shift in preference was a problem for gambling houses and saloons because (regardless of what you see in the movies) poker isn't an ideal casino contest. It doesn't have a house edge, thus a casino cannot earn a profit unless the proprietor charges a seat-fee or takes a portion of every pot.

This was during the industrial revolution, so the solution was inevitably mechanical. Poker machines soon appeared in saloons, cigar stores, and other "dens of iniquity." A typical device had five reels, and each spin of the reels cost one nickel. Prizes were often listed as drinks or cigars to avoid local prohibitions against gambling. One pair of tens or better paid one cigar. Prizes increased for higher hands, and a royal flush paid one hundred cigars…at least theoretically. Few players noticed that five reels with ten reel-positions necessarily excluded two cards, usually ten of spades and jack of hearts. The missing cards and the absence of a draw option dropped the probability of hitting a royal to less than one in one million. Some machines didn't even allow that infinitesimal possibility; the card layout made royals and straight flushes impossible. Ouch!

Nevertheless, poker machines were popular, and the "nickel in the slot" business flourished. As in all emerging growth industries, there were a lot of entrepreneurs creating wacky and off-beat designs. Most used a poker theme. Roulette was also common, but nothing stood out until Charles A. Fey came along and turned the world of slots on its ear. Fey was a Bavarian immigrant who loved to tinker with machines. He lived in San Francisco and built slots part-time in his basement. Fey's designs were so popular he eventually quit his job at an electrical supply business and opened a factory. According to

Fey, the new location was "the best-equipped shop west of the Mississippi."

Apparently so, because in 1899 he created the Liberty Bell slot machine. It had three reels, a handle on the side, and the top combination was three bells in a row. This was something original. A brand new game! The modern slot machine had been born. Two years later Fey built the world's first draw poker machine and presciently called it "the most consistent money maker in counter games that I have known." Talk about predicting the future!

Unfortunately for Fey, the temperance movement was gaining strength at this time, and slot machines were operating in a legal gray area. Fey couldn't get patents for his designs, so he protected his machines by not selling them. He would lease a slot, then personally install the device, and share the profits with the proprietor. That system worked well until one of his machines "disappeared" from a saloon. One year later the Mills Novelty Company introduced the Liberty Bell slot machine. That's right.

Herbert Mills didn't even bother to change the symbols. Fey continued to make slots, but Mills dominated the business for the next forty years.

Cigars, liquor, and coins were considered inappropriate prizes for "trade-stimulating" machines by 1910, so slots ostensibly dispensed gum. Modern-day fruit and bar symbols are a holdover from this era. Remember Bazooka bubble gum? That's the sort of prize you could legally win. The proprietor might give you cash when the cops weren't looking, but these early slots were notoriously tight. The top payout for three bells was only twenty-two coins…uh…I mean bars of gum.

Then along came Prohibition, and slots went the way of alcohol, forced out by the government and straight into the welcoming arms of organized crime. Slots were all the rage in places where they were forbidden, particularly New York where the Mob built a gambling empire.

Fiorello La Guardia, New York City's reform-minded mayor, personally supervised the dumping of 1,200 slots into the

Atlantic Ocean in 1934. One wonders if La Guardia would have been surprised to see, seven decades later, 40,000 machines happily beeping and ringing just down the coast in Atlantic City.

The Depression came and went, and so did World War II, but slots did not fade away. The plucky little machines remained popular. This is ironic because most "serious" gamblers (typically men) looked down their noses at the "one-armed bandits." Slots were for girlfriends and wives, low-rollers, and people down on their luck. Real gambling was (supposedly) only done at tables. And yet, even the most dapper tuxedo-clad player would occasionally stop on his way to or from a table and drop a few coins. There was something cheerful and hypnotic about those happy spinning reels. Slots had a mystical hold on the American psyche.

What they did not have were attractive payoffs and reasonable odds. Twenty coins was still a big jackpot in the mid-twentieth century. Pinball machine manufacturer Bally surveyed the undeveloped market, saw tremendous growth potential, and in 1963 the company debuted an electro-mechanical slot called Money Honey. It had revolutionary new features including a 2,500 coin hopper and a front-opening case. Bally introduced the first three-line machine five years later. The modern slot revolution had begun. Casinos began devoting more floor space to slots.

Slots and poker were reunited in 1976 when Bally launched video poker. This "new" game really took off in 1979 when IGT (then known as Sircoma) released its own updated version of video poker. The public went wild.

Slots and video poker now generate about seventy percent of casino revenue in North America (even more in some locations). And while some stingy machines can still be found, strict regulations and competition make the games generally much more favorable than in years past. Choose your machine wisely and you can play some of the most liberal contests in the gambling world. That's right. Slots can beat the tables. No tuxedo required.

But how can you beat the slots? That's what this book is about.

Part 1

Inside the Machine

Chapter 1

Slots: A Crash Course

SLOT MACHINES HAVE AN AURA OF SIMPLICITY. Drop a coin in the slot, pull the handle or push a button, reels spin, music plays, and you win or lose. Wheeee! The whole process takes just a few seconds.

But this simplicity is only a façade. A typical slot game has billions of variables, and its internal functions are infinitely more complex than poker, blackjack, craps, or any other supposedly "complicated" casino contest. Most of this internal complexity is designed to create random results and prevent you from influencing the game, but happily, not everything is beyond your control. Your choices can significantly affect the outcome of the contest.

In other words, there are slot strategies that work, and you don't need to be a rocket scientist to use them. I'll explain more about that as we go along, but first let's briefly review basic slot machine functions. If you've spent much time in a casino, then the next few paragraphs may be old news, but just in case...

Buttons, Paylines, and Jackpots

When you look past the flashing lights, bells, music, video screens, and other modern paraphernalia, the basic slot game (on the outside) is pretty much the same today as it was a century ago. A typical machine has three or more reels. Each reel has sections that are called **stops**, and every stop is covered with a symbol. It might be cherries, a pot of gold, a Sizzling 7, or something else (sometimes just a blank space).

A player puts a coin or bill into the machine, pulls a handle or pushes a button, and the reels spin. A few seconds later the spinning stops, and the symbols displayed on the reels directly under the **payline** determine how much (if anything) the player has won.

The prizes associated with various reel combinations are displayed on a **pay table** that is on a panel above and/or below the reels. Coins are dispensed into a tray at the bottom of the machine. Some new slots are coinless, and they issue printed vouchers that can be cashed or played in other games.

Standard Slot Machine

Slot games have different designs, but they all have layouts similar to this. Note the pay table on the upper portion of the machine.

Many slots still come with a handle. Pulling it will deliver a wonderfully visceral drag that approximates some designer's idea of how moving gears should feel, but it's just an illusion. The handle performs the same function as the **Spin** button; it activates a separate mechanism that makes the game go.

The **Change** button is used to summon a slot attendant (when the machine runs out of coins or malfunctions). **Cash/Credit** is used to cash out or to switch from receiving coins to receiving machine credits. The latter are displayed on a digital counter.

Bet One wagers credits in single increments. **Bet Max** wagers multiple credits (whatever the machine allows as maximum per spin). Bet Max also activates the spin mechanism.

There's a receptacle for your **players club** card (more on players clubs in Chapter 6), and there's usually a comfy seat where the casino would like you to settle for the next few hours. But don't get too comfortable; the strategies in this book soon will have you moving to a better machine.

GAME TYPES

Slot machines come in various types with many sub-classifications. These distinctions are important because in most cases they indicate how a game should be played for maximum return. I'm going to list them briefly here, and then cover them later in detail.

The casino-industry term "slots" includes **reel-spinners** (often called traditional reels) and video slots. The latter is subdivided

Progressive games come in three types. A wide-area progressive is a game in which many machines at different properties compete for one large, ever-increasing jackpot. An in-house progressive ties machines together at one property. And some stand-alone machines have their own internal progressive jackpot.

into video reels, video poker, video keno, and other video gambling games.

Contests that pay a fixed amount for the top prize are known as **flat tops** or **non-progressive** machines. In contrast, **progressive** games have a top jackpot that grows incrementally each time the game is played.

Many reel games these days have multiple paylines, but you can still find some that have single paylines. Video poker games come in single-hand and multiple-hand versions.

The latest whiz-bang slots have a basic game and a bonus game. One or more of the reel combinations in the basic game will bounce you into a bonus level, and you get to choose something, spin something, and so on.

And finally, some video machines contain multiple games. You can play five different slot games, six different video poker games, blackjack, or keno at one terminal.

Yes, it's a breathtaking cornucopia. It's even more amazing when you consider how similar these machines are on the inside.

THE REEL STORY

Once upon a time the handle on the side of a slot machine actually made the game go. The reels actually decided the outcome of the contest. A player could determine the probability of winning by simply counting the symbols on the reels and doing some basic multiplication.

It was all very straightforward. Unfortunately, it was also very susceptible to fraud. A player could jiggle the handle and control the spin of the reels. Slot manufacturers temporarily solved this problem by separating the handle from the spin mechanism, but thieves simply learned to open the machines and set the reels manually. Other methods of cheating involved drilling holes into a machine to fool it into thinking coins had been deposited, wedging objects into the chute under the coin hopper, or spraying chemicals into the coin slot.

And another problem developed as the twentieth century progressed. Players wanted big jackpots, but big jackpots required longer odds (fewer possibilities of winning the top prize) and that meant more reel stops. Bigger reels needed bigger machines, and that created even more opportunities for cheating. Physical reels were becoming a major liability. Something had to change.

The fundamental shift occurred on May 15, 1984 when Inge Telnaes received U.S. Patent 4,448,419 for an "Electronic Gaming Device Utilizing a Random Number Generator for

Smarter Bet Factoid

Video slots have been around for many years, and their popularity is growing, but traditional reels still garner most of the slot business. Games like Double Diamond, Wheel of Fortune, and Red, White and Blue are consistent favorites.

Selecting the Reel Stop Positions." It was a simple yet stunning leap; put the game on a computer chip. Reel size was no longer an issue. Cheaters setting reels was no longer a problem. Mega-jackpots were possible, and the modern era of slot games had arrived.

By the way, for you tech-heads out there, RNG (the function) and EPROM (the chip) are synonymous in this book.

RNG: The Heart of the Machine

You want to beat a slot machine in the twenty-first century? Then you need to know how a **random number generator** (RNG) works. All slot strategy is based on evaluating these tricky little mechanisms that are at the heart of every modern machine game.

ZERO TO A BILLION

An RNG is a computer chip that randomly selects numbers in a particular range, usually zero to a few billion. Each number is divided using a predetermined formula, and the remainder (the amount left after the division) corresponds to a particular stop on one of the machine's reels.

Yeow! Does that sound complicated? Think of it this way. When you put a coin in the slot and push the spin button, the number that happens to be on the RNG at that particular moment is delivered to a mechanism that controls the reels. The reels spin and give the impression that the contest has yet to be decided, but in fact it's all over. The symbols on the payline simply reflect the numbers selected by the RNG. The handle, buttons, and everything else are just for show.

Not very romantic, huh?

Yes, but an RNG can do amazing things that were never possible with the old reels. Bigger jackpots are just one example. Bonus games are another. And while an RNG is random (by self-definition), it's also programmed to operate within certain parameters.

This is good news for players who use strategy because manufacturers build machines with adjustable rates of return. Casinos use these **loose** (generous) and **tight** (not so generous) games in complex placement strategies to maximize profits, and you can take advantage of those strategies to win more money. It's like buying a cheap airline seat that was sold as a promotion. Meanwhile, the poor schmuck next to you is paying full price.

Loose slots pay
back more on
average than tight
slots, but remember
that short-term
payback tends to be
more volatile than
long-term payback.
So a game may
at first appear to
be tight, but may
actually be loose
(and vice versa).
For more on volatil-
ity, and how to
"read" machines,
see Chapter 3.

THE GAME INSIDE THE GAME

An RNG never stops working. The game is played internally even when the machine is idle. Every millisecond a new number is selected, one after another, forever. That means thousands of losing combinations and hundreds of jackpots are generated in the time it takes you to sit down and push a bill into the machine. Pause for a sneeze or a yawn, and countless decisions will disappear forever into the electronic ether. Hesitate for one-tenth of a second, and you will receive an entirely different game.

This is a very good thing because you never have to worry about missing a jackpot. Just scratch your ear and you've missed a dozen. The results of physical play ARE NOT SEQUENTIAL. They're random. That means a slot machine is never "due" for a hit, and it's never "getting ready to pay off."

In fact, the RNG isn't even aware that money is involved in the contest. RNG operations are entirely indifferent to the number of coins in play or the size of the payoffs. They're also not affected by the presence of a slot club card. The chip is simply oblivious. Nothing you can do to a machine will affect the function of an RNG (short of crushing it with a bulldozer).

RNG AND THE LAW

Every RNG in every slot machine is thoroughly tested and licensed in all *regulated* North American gambling jurisdictions. State laws require that every RNG perform to a certain standard and produce a minimum (or greater) frequency of wins over time. Nevada law requires slots to pay back a minimum of 75% of the money that cycles through the machine. New Jersey requires a minimum 83% payback. Most states (and provinces) are at least as tough as Nevada or tougher. And these regulations are vigorously enforced. For example, every RNG in Atlantic City is individually certified and sealed by New Jersey Division of Gaming Enforcement. A casino cannot alter or replace an RNG except with the following procedure:

- The casino makes an application to the DGE.
- The machine is opened under DGE supervision.
- The DGE breaks the processor's seal and supervises the program/chip replacement.
- The DGE creates a new seal, and re-certifies the machine.

Smarter Bet Factoid

The average payback of a slot machine in Atlantic City is about 92%. The average payback of a slot machine on the Las Vegas Strip is about 94%. The loosest slots in the world can usually be found in North Las Vegas. Machines there typically pay back about 96%.

New Jersey Division of Gaming Enforcement maintains a database of every slot machine in the state. The specific payback percentage of every machine is part of that database. Every RNG is numbered and tracked.

Other states have similar regulations and databases. In Nevada a casino can change an RNG without notifying the state, but it can use only state-approved chips, and the switch must include a paper trail. Inspectors randomly check machines for compliance.

Why should all this matter to you? Because if you find a loose machine tomorrow, it will probably still be loose next month or next year. And you can track that machine by number even if it's moved from one end of the casino to the other. Ditto for avoiding tight machines.

We'll get into the nitty-gritty of tracking loose machines in another chapter, but first we're going to take a closer look at winning and losing, and what you can expect from an RNG.

In Review

🍒 **An RNG (random number generator)** is at the heart of all modern slot machines. This includes machines with traditional reels, video reels, and video poker machines.

🍒 **Every RNG in every slot machine is tested and licensed** in all regulated North American gambling jurisdictions. Laws require that slot machines perform to a particular standard and have a minimum payback.

🍒 **An RNG never stops working.** The game is played internally even when the machine is idle. A new number is selected every millisecond, one after another, forever.

🍒 **RNG operations** are entirely unconnected to the number of coins in play or the size of the payoffs. They're also unconnected to the presence of a slot club card, or any other outside influence.

🍒 **An RNG is random in the short-term, but consistent over time.** This gives a slot machine a particular long-term character. Loose machines are more generous than tight machines.

Chapter 2

The Economics of Gambling

WHY DO COINS FLIP THE WAY THEY DO? Why do cards fall a certain way? What combination of symbols (or cards) will an RNG produce?

This chapter is about probability and how probability works in slots.

If you're not mathematically inclined, don't panic. We won't wade through complicated formulas or graphs. An RNG works a lot like a simple coin toss. Granted, it's a coin toss with a few billion "sides," but any real coin is just as random.

Learning about randomness, probability, and what to expect from coins and computer chips is important because an effective slot machine strategy depends on you being able to reasonably expect certain outcomes. It might seem like magic to the uninitiated, but eventually you will be able to just look at a machine and in most cases know if it is loose or tight. This will be *before* you drop the first coin or push the first bill. Cool, huh?

Yes, but to get to that ninja-like state of expertise we need to go through probability. So let's get started.

Heads vs. Tails, Negative vs. Positive

Take a quarter and flip it. Will George Washington beat the eagle? There's no way to know. That's why they call it a "toss up." Neither side can expect to win one decision or the majority of decisions. A lucky streak could favor George, or the streak could go the other way. A streak may never appear, or there may be many streaks. Anything is possible.

If the payoff on a heads-or-tails wager is 1:1 (even money), then both players have an equal probability of earning a profit or suffering a loss. Remember, a bet requires two opposing persons or entities.

Smarter Bet Factoid
The principles of probability were developed in the seventeenth century by Blaise Pascal and Pierre de Fermat. Pascal had friends who gambled, and he wanted to help them win. Probability is used today for many purposes, such as insurance actuarials and weather forecasting, and we owe it all to gambling.

But let's say the payoff goes higher or lower (1:2, 2:1, etc.). The **true odds** are still 1:1, but the **payoff odds**, or **house odds**, have been shifted. The player who is getting the extra money has a **positive expectation** and the person who is giving the extra money has a **negative expectation**. The difference could be as little as one penny on a dollar wager, but that alone would do it. There is still no way to predict who will win most of the decisions, but one side will inexorably, inevitably, and permanently win more money as the flips continue.

It's a mathematical fact, a rule of the universe. The person wagering the positive side could quit her job and retire if the other guy would just consistently and rapidly keep flipping and betting. This is how casinos earn a profit. They don't have to win all the time. They don't even have to win most of the time; they just need to have a positive expectation. This advantage is commonly known as the **house edge**, and it's usually measured as a percent of the wager.

In the above example a one-penny difference in the payoff (ninety-nine cents paid instead of one-dollar) translates into a 0.5% house edge and a payback to the bettor of 99.5%. In other words, a typical bettor would lose once, win once, and be down an average one cent after two decisions or one-half cent after one decision.

Of course, it's impossible to lose one-half cent; a player either wins 99 cents or loses one dollar. And of course, the flips are random, so there are streaks. A player might win twenty flips out of thirty, or lose thirty of fifty. Anything could happen in a few thousand flips, but over time the player eventually will lose about one-half percent of all the money that is wagered. It doesn't sound like a lot, but those giant palaces in Las Vegas and Atlantic City were built on similar minuscule advantages.

Are all players "doomed" to lose? Not necessarily. Luck plays a role, and so does strategy in some circumstances. But the positive effects of luck and strategy are diminished as the house edge grows. That's why casinos work hard to entice you with games that have a big house edge.

INVENTING A SLOT GAME: CRAZY COINS!

Let's say you're betting on George Washington, and the wager is still one dollar (four quarters). But now we're flipping two coins simultaneously. You get fifteen quarters every time that George appears on both coins. Yay! How often does that happen? About one in four flips.

Fifteen coins is enticing, especially if George hits a streak, but the other bettor

Smarter Bet Tip
Remember that a slot machine keeps your original wager regardless of whether you win or lose, so a two-coin win is actually only one coin if the bet was one coin. And a one-coin win (typical in video poker) is actually a push (a tie).

(the casino) has a 6.25 percent edge in this contest. Number-wonks like me figure it this way:

4 trials x 4 coins per trial = 16 coins invested

16 coins − 15 coins returned = 1 coin of casino profit

1/16 = 6.25% house edge

Wow! Compare this to the original contest. I increased the payout from $1.99 (the $1-dollar bet returned plus a 99-cent win) to $3.75, and I still managed to balloon the house edge from 0.5 percent to 6.25 percent.

But what if you win once, lose once, and then win once more? It's hardly a streak, but that particular combination would put you ahead by eighteen coins. Should the casino be worried? Nope. You or someone else will continue playing the game. Hot and cold streaks will come and go, but the casino will get about a 6.25 percent return on all the **action** (money wagered) as the number of trials stretches into the thousands and then millions.

An actual slot game is just a bit more complicated. We drop some of the payouts to five or ten coins, increase others to twenty, set aside a few extra coins for bigger jackpots, and now we have a new contest: Crazy Coins!

MEASURING THE HOUSE EDGE

The following table, "Good and Bad Casino Bets," gives examples of the house edge on various popular contests. The list goes from best to worst.

Good and Bad Casino Bets

Game	Bet	Casino Advantage
Blackjack	Using basic strategy with counting	-1.00%
Slots: Video Poker	Deuces wild played with optimal strategy	-0.76%
Slots: Video Poker	9/6 played with optimal strategy	0.46%
Blackjack	Using basic strategy with no counting	0.50%
Baccarat	Banker	1.06%
Craps	Pass line	1.41%
Roulette	European wheel with no surrender	2.70%
Slots: Video Poker	8/5 game with optimal strategy	2.70%
Slots: Reels	Flat-top dollar machine (Las Vegas)	5.00%
Roulette	American wheel with no surrender	5.26%
Slots: Reels	Flat-top quarter machine (Atlantic City)	8.00%
Slots: Reels	Progressive	10.0%
Baccarat	Tie	14.4%
Craps	Any seven	16.7%
Keno	Most "big board" bets	30.0%

Blackjack, slots, and keno figures are averages for typical games.

Notice that slot contests cover a wide range. They go all the way from a player edge of 0.76 percent to a casino edge of about 10 percent, and video poker contests pay back more than reel games.

Also, most games are negative expectation for players. It's possible to shift some contests from negative to positive by using an **optimal strategy** (a mathematically optimized system of play), but doing that requires a bit of effort and considerable patience. Remember that the typical advantage remains around one percent or less when it's pushed to the player's side. The house gets a bit more when it has the edge, but most games still earn 5 percent or less. There is no money spigot in a casino. In fact, an often-used phrase from late-night television absolutely applies here; casinos earn money with volume, volume, volume! That's also how advantage players (people who use optimal strategy) do it, too.

You're probably wondering why casinos would offer games that don't give their side a big fat advantage. Why would they play any contests with an edge that could be shifted against them? The answer is somewhat complex and involves public relations and marketing considerations, but it boils down to this; most players don't use optimal strategy. They either don't know that a strategy exists, or they think it's too much trouble to learn. Some people want to be "spontaneous." They prefer to choose whatever game strikes their fancy. Others rely on hunches and superstitions. Whatever the reasons, the result is that typical players win less and lose more on average than optimal-strategy players. Casinos get the PR boost of offering "Certified games that pay back 100%!" But the machines still earn money.

Incredible but true.

The table on the next page, "Cumulative Effects of the House Edge," shows the average expected loss of a regular player compared to an optimal-strategy player.

Of course, anything can happen. The regular player might hit a big jackpot that puts him solidly in the plus column, but consider how much less luck is required for the optimal-strategy player to turn a profit. And it's easy to see which player will last longer if the machines turns cold. Bad luck, good luck, or no luck, the optimal-strategy player will always lose less or win more in the long run.

The RNG and Minimum Payback

But what about this concept of "minimum payback" (required by law) for a slot game? Couldn't the slot be monitored and played only when the RNG is "due" for a hit?

Smarter Bet Tip
If you're interested in learning optimal strategies for poker, blackjack, and craps check out the Smarter Bet Guides to those games.

Cumulative Effects of the House Edge

Number of Decisions (average 10 minutes per 100 spins)	Average Loss for a Regular Player: 8% edge, $1 bets	Average Loss for an Optimal Strategy Player: 1% edge, $1 bets
100	$ 8	$ 1
200	$ 16	$ 2
300	$ 24	$ 3
400	$ 32	$ 4
500	$ 40	$ 5
600	$ 48	$ 6

500 to 600 decisions is approximately one hour of typical slot machine play.

Unfortunately, no. Even if you could read numbers as fast as the Flash, and you had X-ray vision like Superman to monitor every RNG game, it wouldn't help.

Let's return to our humble quarter for the explanation. Forget the payouts. Now we're just interested in heads or tails. The coin is "designed" to deliver heads in about half of the contests. Right? Okay, let's flip. It's tails. Will the coin now "force" heads on the next flip to even the score? No, the probability of seeing heads is still only 50 percent.

What if George hits a bad streak and loses five consecutive times. What's the probability that the streak will extend to six? Should you bet for or against our former commander-in-chief?

Some folks would say that George is "due." Is that right?

No. It's not right. The odds are exactly the same for every flip of the coin.

There are situations when history will affect the future, but in most casino games this is not the case. Here's why:

Deal yourself one card from a deck of cards. You have a 1 in 52 chance of receiving any particular card. Let's say you draw the ten of diamonds. The chance of someone else drawing the ten of diamonds has dropped to zero. In addition, the chance of drawing another red card has dropped to 25 in 51 and the chance of drawing black has increased to 26 in 51. In this situation the first decision (history) will affect subsequent decisions (the future).

Now put the card back and shuffle the deck. The chance of drawing the ten of diamonds is back to 1 in 52. The deck doesn't remember your previous draw.

Spin a roulette ball. Let's say black hits seven consecutive times. Is black now less likely to hit? No. The wheel has no memory.

A random number generator is the same. It is not sentient; it does not respond to history.

So your next spin of the reels is no more or less likely to win than the last spin. You next hand of video poker is no more or less likely to be a royal flush than the last hand. A slot machine can be set to pay back 92 percent over time, but it will almost certainly not return exactly $92 for every $100 played. Let's say the top payout is $1,000 with many smaller jackpots. Some players will see $75 returned. Some might see $85. And a lucky few will win $250, $500, or $1,000. The next contest remains as unpredictable as a coin toss.

EXCEPTIONS, EXCEPTIONS...

But how unpredictable is a coin toss? You don't know what the next decision will be, but you do know that both sides have an equal chance of winning. The odds are 1:1 and not 5:1. That's saying a lot.

Optimal strategy for slot machines is based on this principle. You can't predict the outcome of the next contest, but you can choose the character of the game.

The strategy for video poker goes one step further. You can choose the character of the game, and you *can* make accurate predictions once the cards have been dealt. For example, a low-pair is more likely to produce long-term profit than two face cards.

This additional element of predictability is why optimal strategy works so well on video poker, and that's why video poker returns so much more than typical reel games.

We'll take an in-depth look at video poker in Part 3, but in the next few chapters we're going to focus on slots. I'll tell you how to find loose machines, and we'll debunk some slot machine myths.

In Review

🍒 **Positive-expectation games** are long-term money earners for the person (or entity) playing the positive side. The opposite side of the game has a negative expectation. Most slot contests are negative-expectation games for casino patrons.

🍒 **True odds** are a measure of probability. House odds are a measure of how much a casino will pay on your winning bet. The difference is the house edge, or profit for the casino. A larger edge means the casino has a greater advantage.

🍒 **Optimal strategy** can reduce and in some cases eliminate the house edge.

🍒 **Video poker games** tend to have a lower house edge (higher payback to the player) than reel games.

🍒 **Past results** do not affect the current contest. Inanimate objects do not have memories.

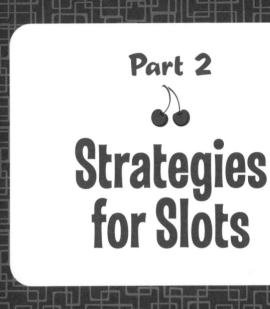

Part 2

Strategies for Slots

Chapter 3

A Loose Machine Is...

PLAYING A SLOT MACHINE IS LIKE STARRING IN YOUR OWN TELEVISION SHOW. Each spin is a five-second episode. There's tension, excitement, resolution, a few laughs, some tears, plenty of cliffhangers, and then the episode ends. What will happen next? The machine is just one big never-ending "must-see" promotion until you start the next game. Of course, winning is the obvious goal, but anticipation keeps people coming back. Everyone loves that delicious feeling when the show is starting and anything can happen. That's why players sit and spin for hours. That's also why so many of the newest games are based on TV shows and movies. In fact, all modern slots have a theme and "story" that plays out in the sequence of wins and losses.

You should know this for two reasons. First, all stories are not alike (and I don't mean Wheel of Fortune is different from Hollywood Squares). Rather, a particular game has a unique character, and it will produce wins with frequencies and in amounts different from other games. Your enjoyment of the contest will be enhanced when you choose a game with payouts that fit your taste.

Second, some games are fundamentally tight, and others are essentially loose. With a little practice you can pretty much look at a machine and know where it will be on the scale. That's what I'll show you how to do in this chapter.

What Makes This Game Different?

A slot machine's unique character begins with the denomination of coins (or base units/credits) it accepts. Nickels, quarters, half-dollars, dollars, and five-dollars are most common, though machines taking other units occasionally can be found. Denomination is one of the most powerful predictors of how a machine will pay back, but before we get into that, let's finish the list of variables.

REELS AND PAYLINES

Reel-spinners are typically three-reel games with one or more paylines. Each payline requires a wager for the line to be active, so playing three lines is essentially the same as playing three games simultaneously (see the illustration on page 41). Games with one, three, five, and nine paylines are common, and a game with multiple paylines can be played with fewer lines than the maximum.

Video reels typically have four or more virtual reels with multiple paylines, but aside from the obvious ability to display animation and bonus games, the practical operation of video slots is identical to reel-spinners.

BUY-A-PAY, MULTIPLIERS, AND PROGRESSIVES

One conceptual variation of multiple paylines is the **buy-a-pay** game. In this situation you're not purchasing additional paylines, but you're buying the opportunity to hit additional winning combinations. In other words, three bars are worth 50 credits and three sevens are worth nothing if you wager one dollar, but two dollars will "activate" the sevens, and they'll be worth 100 credits if they hit.

Another conceptual variation of this is a **bonus multiplier.** It's one of those industry terms that often confuses more than it explains. A standard **multiplier** game pays exact multiples of whatever amount is wagered. Smack the top prize with one credit and you win 500. Whack it with two credits and you win 1,000. It's simple multiplication. A bonus multiplier adds a bonus to the top prize when a player wagers maximum credits.

Multiple Paylines

Each payline requires a separate wager. The game can be played with wagers on fewer than all the lines.

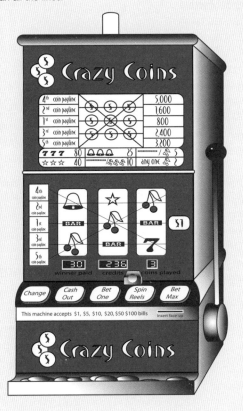

Smarter Bet Factoid

Hit frequency for slot machines is typically between 8 and 33 percent. Reel-spinners usually hit less often than video slots, but it depends on the game and the number of lines in play. A game that hits frequently is not necessarily loose, especially if most wins are less than the value of the wager.

Buy-a-pay and bonus multipliers are taken to an extreme with progressive machines. A portion of every dollar you wager builds the top prize, and it's often worth millions. The pay table has a meter showing the current value of the big jackpot, and there's usually another large display meter above the machine. A player must wager the maximum per spin to be eligible for the top prize. Imagine the horror of playing one coin, hitting the magic combination, and missing a multi-million dollar payoff. Sadly, this happens from time to time. Inevitably, there's a big commotion and an angry player will demand to know why he's not entitled to a mega-jackpot.

HIT FREQUENCY AND VOLATILITY

Hit frequency is a measure of how often a machine pays out. Volatility measures the relative value of those payouts over time. A machine with high volatility will hold a lot for a while, and then pay out a lot very quickly (or vice versa). A low-volatility game will return its payback percentage in less time. High hit frequency and high volatility are not necessarily mutually exclusive, but they do tend to occupy opposite ends of the spectrum. Game designers know that some slot players simply want "time on the machine;" these players aren't necessarily seeking a life-changing top prize. Other gamblers specifically want the thrill of pulling for a fortune. The former group tends to prefer high-hit frequency games with video screens and things like that. The latter group is willing to sacrifice some hit frequency for a shot at the gold.

BONUS GAMES, WILD PAY, AND OTHER GIMMICKS

Every game has a gimmick, something intended to separate it from the crowd. A typical gimmick is one or more bonus levels. A player hits a particular reel combination and the game goes into bonus mode. It can be as simple as a spinning wheel for Wheel of Fortune, or as complex as a round of Yahtzee.

Another common gimmick is wild symbols that double, triple, quintuple, or otherwise increase the payout of any reel combination. Wild symbols also sometimes **nudge**; they hit just above or below the payline, and then they click into position. Hurrah! But of course, this cliffhanger is just for show. The winning combination was predetermined when you pressed the button.

Some machines have wild symbols that make them go bonkers; the game spins and hits many times without requiring extra coins.

The Casino's Big Picture

Here's how the cornucopia of variables affects a machine's payout.

The gaming industry is like movies, theme parks, cruising, and other leisure industries; that is, it's all about selling entertainment. Everything is measured by long-term profit. Casino managers don't care very much about winning or losing individual decisions. In fact, they absolutely love to give away huge jackpots. And they certainly don't want to "take all your money." That would be horrible because it would make you unhappy, and you might not come back next week, next month, or next year.

Casino managers would prefer that you play for a very long time, win some, and lose a bit more than you win. Meanwhile, you're eating in the restaurants, seeing the shows, and generally enjoying the casino's party atmosphere. Of course, the idea of smacking a big jackpot never entirely leaves your mind, so you find yourself drifting back to the

Smarter Bet Factoid

The gaming industry in the United States generates more revenue than the combined income from movies, the music business, theme parks, and organized sports: over $60 billion every year. And that's gaming only. The figure doesn't include income from restaurants, shows, shops, and other peripheral businesses.

Typical Slot Machine Payouts
by percent

Jurisdiction	5¢	25¢	50¢	$1	$5
Atlantic City	89.9	91.6	91.4	92.5	95.2
Connecticut	90.5	91.2	90.8	91.7	94.2
Las Vegas Strip	91.6	93.0	94.3	94.6	95.6
Las Vegas Downtown	91.9	95.0	95.9	95.5	96.9
North Las Vegas	93.4	96.8	98.0	97.6	NA
Mississippi North River	90.3	92.3	93.7	95.2	96.0
Mississippi Coast	91.9	93.0	94.5	95.0	94.9
Reno	93.4	94.6	92.8	95.9	96.9

The above figures are percent payback averages from totals reported in the winter of 2002. They include slots and video poker. Notice that higher-denomination games are generally looser.

machines. And if you don't hit big this trip, maybe next time. See? You're already planning another visit.

Of course, everyone is different. Some people are day-trippers. Others play once a year. There are neophytes and regulars. The wide variety of machines and payouts is designed to maximize long-term profit from every type of customer, and to keep them coming back.

ALL MACHINES MUST PULL THEIR WEIGHT

A nickel machine requires the same amount of electricity, maintenance, and floor space as a machine that takes dollars. Yes, cheaper contests are designed to attract low-budget players, but the games still must earn a profit. Lower-denomination games do this by being tighter than higher-denomination games. Nickel slots are typically tighter than quarter slots. Quarters are tighter than dollars. Dollars are tighter than five-dollar games, and so on (see the chart on page 45). There are exceptions to this rule, but not many.

SIZE MATTERS

Big jackpots are created by reducing the size or frequency of smaller payoffs, so the tightest machines are usually million-dollar progressives. Similar math applies to flat-top machines with large top jackpots. Generally, your chance of hitting the big prize goes up when the size of that prize goes down, and mid-size jackpots become easier to hit, too.

LOCATION, LOCATION, LOCATION

The title of this section isn't a repeat of the old real estate maxim. Location actually applies in three different ways.

First, slots are looser in some jurisdictions. For example, slots are typically two to four percent looser in Las Vegas than in Atlantic City. Slots are tighter on the Las Vegas Strip than in downtown Las Vegas. Slots in Reno are generally looser than those in Connecticut. Competition and the character of the local market cause these variances. When you consider that the entire population of the northeast U.S. is served by slightly more than one dozen "local" casinos, and that all of them could fit into a couple miles of the Las Vegas Strip with room left over, it's easy to understand why Las Vegas slots are loose.

Second, slots tend to be tighter at upscale properties, particularly those frequented by tourists. Games are generally looser when a property is older or when it caters to the local crowd. Thus Bellagio is generally tighter than Sam's Town in Las Vegas.

Third, a game's placement in the casino is a big indicator of how it will play. In fact, it's such a big indicator that the information deserves its own section.

Evaluating the Casino Layout

Slot machines are not positioned willy-nilly in a casino. There's a definite structure and a thought process that governs their arrangement. In the old days loose machines were near entrances, and the sound of falling coins would lure players in. Since those machines were occupied, new players would move further into the casino and play tighter machines. Clever, but more sophisticated and improved placement strategies have emerged in the last few decades.

Here's an overview of what a casino executive is thinking when the layout plan is developed:

SLOTS AND TABLES

Table players don't like ringing bells and other distracting noise because it tends to slow the game and it creates confusion. Also, table players who pass by or through a row of slots sometimes play a few coins just for kicks. But they rarely spend more. Table players prefer tables. On the other hand, a slot-playing spouse or friend of a table player will often play a nearby machine if the person at the table is at the end of a session (they're waiting to go to a show or dinner).

So slots near tables are generally tight to cut down on noise and because most people who play those games will be doing it spontaneously without any big expectation of winning. The machines are there to suck up loose change and extra bills, not necessarily to draw someone in for a long session.

SLOT PLAYER PSYCHOLOGY

In contrast to table players, slot players love to see and hear people winning on the machines. They are pulled like moths to light when a nearby game repeatedly hits. Ringing bells and dropping coins are absolute "proof" that the games can be beaten, so a typical slot player is more likely to play faster and stay longer when people are winning nearby.

Slot layouts take advantage of this by putting the loosest machines in highly visible areas that are deep inside the layout (rather than on the edges). Crosswalks, elevated sections, and places at or near the end of rows are where the most liberal machines are placed. But beware, loose machines are invariably surrounded by tighter games (though not necessarily the tightest). It's typical to have one or two 98 percent machines that are easily visible, and they'll be surrounded by games somewhere in the range of 88 percent to 95 percent.

TIGHT, TIGHTER, TIGHTEST

Tight machines are mostly squeezed back into corners and areas where players are pushed when the casino is full. Consider the typical person who arrives on a busy Friday or Saturday night. It's like parking spaces; the convenient spots are taken, so the player heads farther into corners of the layout to find an available machine. That game is invariably tight.

Smarter Bet Tip
Two games can be identical on the outside but set to pay back differently on the inside. This is especially true when the two games are in different casinos. Don't assume that Double Diamond in casino A will necessarily pay the same as Double Diamond in Casino B.

Slots near a hotel's front desk, a line for a show, a restaurant, or any other waiting area, are similar to the machines near tables. The audience is essentially captive, so the games are usually not generous.

Big Bertha machines (the giant games with the oversized reels) will be played regardless of their payoff, so they're notoriously tight. Ditto for any novelty game that people will play just to see the reels spin.

The tightest of the tight slots can be found in non-casino venues like airports, gas stations, and convenience stores. The Brake-n-Buy is not competing with a casino, and it doesn't care about generating slot excitement. A few occasional quarters from bored patrons is the lone goal.

The same applies to a riverboat or Native-American casino that doesn't have competition nearby. Tight games are more common when the customers are essentially captive.

Of course, tight doesn't mean impossible. Any game that operates within legal specifications will occasionally provide a nice jackpot, but remember that the difference between 83 percent and 98 percent isn't just 15 percent more for the casino. It's also a 750 percent increase in a player's long-term loss.

So now you know the basics of finding loose slots. In the next chapter we're going to expand on these basics, and we'll organize them into a unified strategy. Also, we'll review some additional tools that will help you find profitable games.

In Review

🍒 **Denomination** is one of the biggest indicators of how a slot machine will pay. Higher-denomination machines tend to be looser.

🍒 **The loosest slots** are placed in highly visible areas near the center of a slot layout. They're always surrounded by tighter machines (but not necessarily the tightest).

🍒 **Tight machines** are usually found at the edges of the slot layout in corners and other low-visibility areas. These are places where people will play when the casino is crowded.

🍒 **Machines tend to be tight near table games,** show lines, check-in lines, and restaurant waiting areas.

🍒 **The tightest slots** can be found in airports, convenience stores, and other non-casino venues.

🍒 **Slots are looser in jurisdictions where** many casinos compete for customers. The games also tend to be looser in older properties, and casinos that cater to locals.

Chapter 4

How to Find Loose Slots

SLOTS ARE SUPPOSED TO BE FUN, RIGHT? What's the point of playing if you're not having fun?

Of course, losing money isn't too much fun, but one person's entire bankroll might be an amount that another player tips for drinks. Losses are relative. So ask yourself this: in the pursuit of convenience and unbridled slot fun, is it okay if you spend an extra $1,000 or $2,000 during your next casino visit? Will you finish the session happy? To anyone who answers yes, I offer this advice: forget strategy. Cut loose and go wild!

But if your idea of fun does *not* include losing ten or twenty Ben Franklins, if you'd like to save that money and give yourself a better chance of hitting a jackpot, then the information in this chapter absolutely applies to your situation.

I mention this because the strategies presented here require effort. They're not complicated or difficult, but it's like servicing a car or practicing a golf swing; you've got to actually do it to see the results.

The good news (besides losing less and winning more) is that using optimal strategy can be one of the most enjoyable parts of the game. Hunting for loose machines is often fun as well as potentially profitable.

Choose the Right Casino

Licensed casinos in North America are required to report the *actual* payback percentages of their slot machines to regulators. That information is available to the public in most states and in Canada. Thankfully, you don't have to call a dozen different agencies to get those numbers. They're collected, organized, and published in the magazines *Casino Player* and *Strictly Slots*.

For example, I can tell you that the numbers in March 2002 show that Sands had the loosest five-dollar slots in Atlantic City. They returned a generous 97 percent on average. The tightest five-dollar slots were at Caesars; they paid only 94 percent. The absolute tightest slots in Atlantic City were at Bally's and Harrah's. The nickel machines at those casinos paid a stingy 89.2 percent.

The figures are published monthly and they vary a bit over time, so you shouldn't absolutely judge a casino by one chart, but I can tell you that Harrah's nickels were tightest in January and February, too. Read the charts for a few months and it's easy to see which casinos and machines are consistently looser.

Casino Player and *Strictly Slots* are published by Casino Publishing Group. You can subscribe via the web at www.casinocenter.com or by telephone: 1-800-969-0711. Both magazines are also available at major newsstands and bookstores.

Define Your Game

Slot charts are an important first step, but they have limitations. They don't tell you where the best games are in a casino, and in some jurisdictions the numbers are published by region rather than property. For example, the charts show that North Las Vegas is looser than the Strip, but they don't say how Texas Station stacks up against the Flamingo.

Another limitation of the charts is that video poker is included in the numbers. As you know, video poker (played with optimal strategy) has a significantly higher payback, and that tends to skew the figures upward.

So the next step in slots optimal strategy is a personal choice. Where do you want to play? What games do you like?

You already know the variables. But how will you apply them? Here are some options to consider.

NICKELS VS. HIGHER DENOMINATIONS

Many of the hottest new games take nickels. Nine lines multiplied by five coins per-line is forty-five coins per spin or $2.25. A typical player will do about 500 spins per hour. That's $1,125 of action (money cycled through the machine). With 90 percent payback on average, the action will result in a loss of about $112 unless a player hits one or more good jackpots.

Compare this to playing max coins on a three-line dollar machine that pays back 94 percent. The action is $3 per spin, $1,500 per hour, but the casino keeps only $90 on average. Fewer jackpots are needed to break even or pull ahead. This advantage is even more pronounced if you play a one-dollar game that takes two credits max.

Of course, you could always play single coins in a nickel machine. That would

Slot machine optimal strategy differs from video poker optimal strategy because the latter is absolute; there is only one way to correctly play a video-poker hand (the cards and the pay table determine the strategy). In contrast, reel games have unknown variables, so optimal strategy requires some informed guesses.

be $25 of action in an hour at a total cost of $2.50. Very cheap, but also kind of boring. Most of the wins would be less than one dollar.

SHOOT FOR THE MOON?

Do you love pulling for millions? Then by all means, shoot for the moon. But remember that a typical progressive game of any denomination is comparable in tightness to a nickel machine, usually 90 percent payback or worse. And the probability of hitting the top prize on a million-dollar progressive is microscopically small.

While we're on the subject of big versus little, let's talk about the allure of tight mega-casinos versus the frugal advantages of smaller properties. Do you want chandeliers and tapestries hanging overhead while you pull for a seven-digit jackpot, or will standard track-lights and chain-restaurant-style decorations suffice? What if a casino has loose slots but lousy restaurants? What if the games are good but the drink service is slow? What if your friends want to go to the fancy place?

As you can see, there's no absolutely correct answer to any of these questions. It's all a matter of taste, preference, and your budget. But remember that optimal strategy for slot machines is only as optimal as you make it. With that caveat, here's the pure strategy. You can pick and choose what works best for you.

Prep for the Session

First, all things being equal, you should always opt to play video poker. Take another look at the chart on page 29. Almost any video poker game will pay back more over time than a typical slot machine. So unless your heart is set on reels, go with video poker.

Still want to spin for gold? Fine. The next step is to determine the size of your bankroll.

MANAGING YOUR MONEY WITH A BANKROLL

Let's say you start a **session** with $500 and finish with $800. That's a $300 profit. Pretty good, right? But what if I told you that you had $2,500 halfway through the session? $300 doesn't sound so good anymore because you lost $1,700!

Most people use a **bankroll** (money set aside specifically for wagering) when they gamble. Unfortunately, the average player doesn't plan much farther than that. The bankroll is treated as a simple **stop-loss**, that is, the gambling stops when the money is gone. **Win-limits** (plans for locking up profits and leaving the casino) are nonexistent or vaguely defined. The accounting at the end of the session for the typical player is simply plus or minus, up or down.

That system is fine for a casino that has unlimited funds and a positive expectation, but it's a one-way ticket to a busted bankroll for players on the negative-expectation side.

ROLLING STOP-LOSS

A **rolling stop-loss** is a more sophisticated method of handling stop-losses and win-limits than the typical "stop when you lose it all" rule. It also prevents the disappointment of being significantly up and then losing it all back.

A rolling stop-loss can be any amount you choose, and there are various ways of calculating it, but the "sliding window" is pretty typical. Let's say I start a session with 100 units (dollars, coins, whatever) and my window is 100. If I win 50 then the window slips forward by that amount. The original stop-loss was zero units. The new stop loss has moved forward to 50. I will always exit the session if I lose 100 units from the highest point of my bankroll. That means I'm permanently in the black when I go past 200 units.

Keep in mind that this system works by limiting action and bankroll volatility. It's a practical way of managing your money, but it doesn't change the house edge. Wager-for-wager you won't win any more or less on average than someone who never stops playing until the bankroll is exhausted, but if losing is in your future, you'll go there slowly.

Also remember, a rolling stop-loss is part of a larger strategy; your big plan is to survive short-term fluctuations and thus have more opportunities to smack a big prize.

STANDARD BET AND SESSION BANKROLL

Choose an amount that you feel comfortable wagering per spin. It can be a quarter, a dollar, five dollars, whatever. Keep in mind that this isn't about the denomination of games you'll play. This is an internal choice. How much per spin? Let's use one dollar as an example. We'll call that your standard bet.

Your session bankroll should be at least 150 times the one dollar standard bet or $150. Five dollar bets should have a

Smarter Bet Tip

One alternative to a rolling stop-loss is a once-through method of wagering. You risk each unit (or group of units) exactly once. A net loss ends the session. A net win is divided into thirds. The original bankroll and one-third of the win is permanently set aside. The remaining money is wagered again using the once-through method.

Increase your session bankroll to 200 times the standard bet if the units are less than one dollar. This gives you more chances to win on tighter nickel and quarter games.

$750 or greater session bankroll. Remember, this is gambling, so you should be prepared to lose it all. Though it would be unlikely that you could nuke the whole amount in one session unless you seriously deviate from optimal strategy, jackpots happen, and so do losing streaks. Keep in mind that slots are a negative-expectation game; you're *supposed* to lose in the long run. Optimal strategy is designed to reduce those losses and give you more chances to hit a big jackpot.

Each session will be about one to two hours. Two sessions a day is typical for most players. If you prefer to calculate your bankroll on a per-day basis, set aside at least 250 bets (notice that the variance goes down gradually as the time and trials increase).

Optimal Strategy in Action

Okay, it's time to hit the machines.

Choose a casino and a loose area of that casino as described in Chapter 3.

This is important. The following system won't work if you play tight machines. Well, actually, it will work because it will quickly stop you from playing. But the point of this system is to increase your chance of winning, so you should choose the right area.

Progressive games are out. Just walk right past them. You'll have plenty of time to dump a few dollars into Wheel of Fortune or Megabucks later (if your current session goes well).

Stick to flat tops. The exact game types are entirely up to you. Video or physical reels are fine. Ditto for single or multiple paylines. Try to find games with a top jackpot lower than 10,000 coins/credits. Less than 5,000 is even better.

You should bet the maximum in the highest-denomination machine where a maximum wager matches your standard bet, but do this only if the game pays a bonus for the extra coins. If it does not pay a bonus, then find a similar game in an even higher denomination and play single credits.

Smarter Bet Tip

The best time to play slots is when a casino is relatively empty. Fewer players will be competing for the loosest machines. Avoid weekends, holidays, and major conventions. Mornings and afternoons are typically better than evenings.

You won't be able to exactly match your standard bet size all the time, but try to stay in a reasonable range. A one-dollar per-spin bet can shrink to seventy-five cents or expand to $1.25, but two dollars is too high, and fifty cents is too low.

AND AWAY WE GO!

Pick a machine that looks juicy and load it with ten bets (your standard units, not machine credits). Spin ten times. If you don't get a hit, move to another machine. Repeat the process. When you do get one or more hits (and you soon will if you've chosen the right section of the casino to play), continue playing until you either hit zero or go over twenty bets on the meter. If you go over twenty, cash out and reload with ten bets.

Always exit the machine when you hit zero or when the amount on the meter is less than your standard bet. Don't hesitate, just cash out and move on.

If the machine keeps you going for a while, then you've probably found a loose one. Record the machine's number and write a detailed description of the machine's denomination, game, and location so you can find it again. Did I mention that you should be carrying paper and a pen?

The purpose of this system is to get you off tight machines, and off machines that are bleeding you dry with small wins and a high hit frequency. You'll either stay with a machine and earn money, or walk away with a ten-unit or less loss.

This system will make some casinos and/or areas of casinos unplayable. Good! You shouldn't be feeding coins into tight machines.

Stop after an hour or two. You should have a profit or a small loss (part of your bankroll should still be intact). If you lost most of your money, or you finished the bankroll in less than an hour, then you were playing in the wrong casino or the wrong section of the casino. Don't play there again.

Keep good records, and you'll eventually build a list of loose machines. A picture will emerge of the loose/tight layout like a connect-the-dots puzzle. Soon you'll be walking straight to the loose slots.

MODIFYING THE SYSTEM

The money management system in the previous section can be modified to accommodate your personal style and the games you like to play. For example, low hit-frequency games are more playable when you increase the spin cycles from

Smarter Bet Tip
Every machine has a multiple-digit identification number somewhere on its exterior. The number is unique to that machine. Having the number will help you find it again if it's moved to another section of the layout.

Smarter Bet Tip

Keep your eyes and ears open when looking for loose slots. If you see someone winning a lot (or losing a lot) on a particular machine, note that machine and adjust your strategy accordingly.

ten bets to twenty and you double the buy-in. But of course, that puts more money at risk on one machine. It's a personal choice.

Other modifications that are more conservative include lowering the cash-out-and-reload threshold to fifteen bets and lowering the buy-in from ten bets to eight or seven. These two adjustments will move you through machines very quickly. Games will either produce profit, or you're out of there. When they do give you some money, you'll lock it up.

WHEN IN DOUBT, CASH OUT

Remember that cashing out is not a bad thing. It's perfectly okay to load the machine, play one spin, and then decide you don't want to be there anymore. Just hit the cash button, collect your money, and move on. Let's say a machine has been stringing you along for ten minutes, and it never quite reaches an upper limit or zero. Stay with it if you're having fun, but cash out if you're tired of the stalemate. Yes, one spin more might nail you a big jackpot, but saving that spin for another better machine might give you an even bigger win. Let your instinct guide you at these borderline moments.

By the way, you probably noticed that this strategy has you moving around the casino a lot. That's a good thing. You won't get too "invested" (emotionally or otherwise) in one machine unless it's generous. Also, walking around will give you a better sense of the layout.

A Progressive Look At Progressives

Traditional progressive games build the top jackpot with a portion of every wager, usually through a system that links multiple machines, but in the last few years a new type of single-machine progressive bonus has been developed. Games that use this bonus structure are typically called **banking games**. The machine slowly builds credits in an internal bank that is separate from the top jackpot. Some of these games include Big Bang Piggy Bankin', Double Diamond Mine, Fort Knox, and Buccaneer Gold.

Keep in mind that all progressives of any type (including Megabucks) have a mathematical break-even point where the value of the jackpot is large enough to make the game a positive-expectation wager. We'll explore this in depth in the video poker section, but the important point here is that you have to hit the jackpot for the equation to work. That's very unlikely when the odds are in the millions, but it's more likely with a banking game.

Unfortunately ten, twenty, or even fifty spins generally won't do it; you've got to settle in for the long haul, at least eighty to one hundred spins. And of course, the game has to have enough credits in the bank to make it worth chasing.

If you're going to sit down at a machine and play for a while, then I strongly suggest that you make it video poker. But if you happen to find a reel game with a bank that is unusually large or near capacity, then go ahead and give it a shot. Just don't be disappointed if you haven't smacked the bank after one hundred spins or more. By the way, most banks are worth less than $100 (depending on the denomination).

On the Other Hand

There are some places where you simply won't find any loose slots because a lack of competition or restrictive state regulations keep the machines tight. For example, the law in West Virginia requires all machines to pay back no more than 95 percent, and games in that state usually pay back less than 92 percent. So evaluating the layout at Charles Town Races is a waste of time. Ditto for a Native American casino or riverboat that has a lock on the local gambling business. And you won't find a loose nickel machine at Mandalay Bay or Venetian. These are just a few examples of venues where the games are uniformly mediocre or tight.

In Review

🍒 **Slot paybacks** for most casinos in North America are published monthly in the magazines *Casino Player* and *Strictly Slots*.

🍒 **Slot machine optimal strategy** is only as optimal as you make it. Your choices affect the probability of success.

🍒 **A session bankroll** should be at least 150 times the size of your standard bet. This reduces the possibility that an unlucky streak will prematurely end your session.

🍒 **The purpose of optimal strategy and money management** is to get you off tight machines, and off machines that are bleeding you dry with small wins and a high hit frequency.

🍒 **Remember that cashing out is not a bad thing.** It's perfectly okay to load the machine, play one spin, and then decide you don't want to be there anymore.

🍒 **All things being equal,** you should play video poker instead of reel games.

Chapter 5

Hitting the Big One

HERE'S SOMETHING THAT YOU WON'T SEE IN A TYPICAL BOOK ABOUT SLOT MACHINES. It's an entire chapter devoted to the consequences of winning. This isn't cheerful optimism; it's a practical truth. You will win if you play long enough. It's mathematically inevitable.

Your gambling life, from a statistical point of view, is one long session separated by breaks for work and other activities. For example, you can expect to see a royal flush jackpot (typically 4,000 credits when using optimal strategy) about once in every 110 hours of single-hand video poker. You may play that much in a few weeks, or it may take months or years, but if you continue playing then it will happen. The probability goes up considerably when you play multiple hands/paylines. The jackpot might be a giant windfall or a smaller amount that simply erases a fraction of your aggregate losses, but either way, you want to keep it. You don't want it delayed or disallowed. It's coming, and you've earned it. So don't stick your head in the sand. Prepare now.

What Could Go Wrong?

Minor jackpots are no big deal. A bunch of credits appear on the meter, you cash out and buy yourself something fancy. Nice. But things change considerably when a jackpot is large enough to require a **hand-pay** (a cash or check payment from a casino employee). Hand-pays occur for two reasons: either a machine can't pay enough coins, or the win exceeds a tax reporting threshold of $1,200 or more.

Both situations require a casino employee to give you and the machine some degree of scrutiny. Frankly, amounts less than $1,200 receive little attention unless something is suspicious. On the other hand, once you go over that magic number...well...read on and see for yourself.

Smarter Bet Factoid
Casinos in the United States use IRS form W2G to report jackpots of $1,200 and over. Amounts under $5,000 are reported, but they're not subject to federal withholding when the player provides a social security number. Amounts above $5,000 require 28 percent withholding when the payoff is more than 300 times greater than the wager.

WHO ARE YOU?

First, you should understand the strict legal atmosphere in which gambling transactions are conducted in the United States. Every wager is regulated by thousands of laws that describe to the very smallest detail exactly what is permissible and what is forbidden. Casinos that break the rules are fined, sometimes heavily. Repeated offences can endanger an operating license, so casinos will strictly follow government rules (as opposed to their own, which they may bend) no matter how much you protest. It's not about PR; it's about staying in business.

One of the most important rules involves U.S. tax law and slot machine jackpots of $1,200 and up. Winners must provide identification and a social security number or 31 percent of the jackpot will be withheld for federal taxes. No exceptions. Ever.

In many U.S. jurisdictions the casino will withhold the entire amount if you are unable to provide identification. That's right. No ID? No money. Nevada is marginally more flexible. You might get the remaining 69 percent without identification in some casinos, or you might not. Charlie Lombardo, Senior VP for slot operations at Caesar's Palace in Las Vegas, calls it "discretionary" depending on the circumstances of the win. "If I see a problem then I ask for ID."

The most accepted form of identification is a driver's license with your picture. Military ID and the like are also suitable, but voter registration cards, credit cards, a hunting license, or your grocery card won't cut the mustard.

People without identification are photographed, and the casino holds the money until they return with the necessary documents (additional withholding applies in various circumstances). No amount of pleading, tears, or threats will influence casino managers to bend these rules.

MINOR PROBLEMS

Dolores Banyai was thrilled when she pressed the button and hit a $220,200 jackpot on a Wheel of Fortune machine at the Hilton in Atlantic City. Unfortunately, she was only nineteen years old and the minimum legal age for gambling in New Jersey is twenty-one. A slot attendant appeared and requested identification. Banyai realized her age would be a problem, so she got sneaky. She said her ID was in a hotel room. Banyai then pressed her twenty-one-year old boyfriend, David Baum, into service, and he returned later to claim the jackpot. This happened over a matter of hours, and there was a shift change, so the casino paid the prize. But what these youngsters didn't count on is that every large jackpot is videotaped, and the tape is checked for verification. In this case, it took longer than it should have to catch the mistake, but the result was inevitable. The casino realized what had happened, and they immediately contacted the New Jersey Division of Gaming Enforcement.

States where the minimum gambling age is twenty-one include Nevada, New Jersey, New Mexico, Mississippi, Missouri, Maryland, Indiana, Delaware, Colorado, Connecticut, North Dakota, South Dakota, and South Carolina. Legislation to raise the minimum age to twenty-one is pending in other states, so anyone under twenty-one should check before playing.

The state filed criminal charges. Banyai lost the jackpot and she was fined. Her boyfriend was indicted on one count of theft by deception (prosecutors later dismissed the charge). The casino was fined $10,000.

The minimum gambling age varies by jurisdiction, so some gamblers are not even aware (or perhaps are willfully ignorant) that they cannot wager legally in Nevada, New Jersey, Mississippi and many other places until they're twenty-one. But they inevitably become very aware moments after hitting the $1,200 threshold, or any time a win requires a casino employee to hand-pay. Underage players are not paid jackpots. There are no exceptions. No amount of legal wrangling has ever changed that anywhere in the U.S. Just ask Russell Erickson. His son Kirk was nineteen when he hit for $1 million at Caesars Palace. First they tried the switch, and that didn't work. Then Russell sued, but the jackpot was disallowed.

Switching with an older person is a common ploy that fails miserably every time. Sometimes the winner just walks away. But the end result is always the same, a heartbreaking loss. Underage gamblers can't win.

FRIENDS DON'T LET FRIENDS SHARE JACKPOTS

"This one's for you, Puddin'." That's what Mary Iacono remembers Carolyn Lyons saying just before Carolyn pushed the button. Seconds later the slot machine delivered a jackpot of $1.9 million. Mary was ecstatic because she thought half the money was hers, but that's not how it worked out.

The two women were vacationing together in Las Vegas, and (according to Mary) they made an agreement to split their winnings. Mary says Carolyn even paid for the trip because she thought her friend would be "lucky" for both of them.

They were down $47 and late for a show when Mary (who uses a wheelchair) begged her friend to stop on the way out and play once more. Carolyn resisted but eventually gave in. The big one came on the second spin.

"Whoever pushes the button and initiates the game is the winner," says Frank Kersh, slot manager at Horseshoe, Tunica. He states it flatly and without equivocation. That's the legal rule, and everybody in the casino business follows it. A winner can certainly share a jackpot, but only one person is the winner.

In this case the winner was Carolyn, and she didn't share. Mary claimed they had an oral contract. She sued. Headaches and heartache for everyone.

The lesson here is that you should play your own game. It might seem romantic for one person to drop the coins and another to press the button, but unless you have a written agreement of some sort (or you're married) then you're playing with slots, and also playing with fire.

PAY NO ATTENTION TO THE RAM BEHIND THE CURTAIN

One of the surest ways to "lose" a jackpot is to psych yourself into thinking that you've won a big prize when in fact the machine has simply malfunctioned. Too many people spend years of their lives litigating such "stolen" prizes, and they usually come up short. Here's how it happens. You're playing a progressive. The symbols line up, lights flash, bells ring, but something is wrong. The progressive meter hasn't reset. People may already be congratulating you on your good fortune, but a slot technician checks the machine and eventually the bad news arrives. The machine malfunctioned. "But the symbols lined up," you sputter. "That's a jackpot. Who cares if some electrical doodad didn't send a signal? The reels told me I had a jackpot! I won $10 million!"

You didn't. That "electrical doodad" is the RNG. Think of the reels like the scoreboard at the Super Bowl. The stadium display helps you understand who is winning, but it has no bearing on the game.

What could cause a slot machine to malfunction? Designers and regulators go to extreme lengths to insure that slots operate properly, but in spite of that they sometimes break. Problems include corrupted RAM (random access memory), power interruptions, reel malfunctions, or just a bug in the program. The latter happened to Nhung Housekeeper. She was playing a progressive at Spirit Mountain Casino in Oregon and hit a $2.9 million jackpot. Unfortunately, it was a nickel machine with a top payout that should have been only $10,000. The casino refused to pay. Here come the lawyers!

When is a Jackpot a Jackpot?

There is more to a jackpot than reels and ringing bells. A genuine win includes a combination of external indicators that you can see immediately, and there are some internal items that can only be

Smarter Bet Factoid
Look closely, and you'll see that slot machines are labeled with the phrase, "Malfunctions void all pays and plays." It's like buying a soda. Let's say the soda machine breaks and fifty sodas come out. You're entitled to one soda, not fifty.

checked by the casino. Remember, the following are all indicators. The only thing that really matters is the RNG.

Of course, it starts with the reels or display. You should see
a winning combination. Next, the machine must lock up. If it
doesn't, then you don't have a hand-pay jackpot. The lock-up
feature insures that you won't accidentally "play away" your big
win. The **tower light** should be on and in many cases it should
not be flashing (it depends on the game). Bells should be ringing
continuously. If the contest is progressive and you hit the big
prize, then the progressive meter should reset. If any of the above
indicators are missing then you probably have a malfunction. If
everything appears correct then get ready to be excited, but don't
celebrate just yet.

VERIFYING A JACKPOT

A casino representative should approach you within a few minutes after you hit (though it may seem like an eternity). Some
casinos are slower than others, especially on weekends. Once
someone arrives you'll do the ID thing. Jackpots under
$10,000 are paid with little fanfare. Amounts above that
receive a higher level of scrutiny. The casino will check surveil-
lance cameras to be sure that you were the person playing the
machine. They'll also run the tape back to see if the machine
was rigged before it paid off. Don't feel insulted; scams are a
problem.

If the win was on a wide-area progressive then an additional inspection occurs. Casinos don't pay progressive jackpots when games are linked to multiple properties (as in Megabucks). The slot manufacturer handles those payments. The casino notifies the manufacturer when a jackpot hits, and company representatives come out to examine the machine and cut a check.

How is a machine examined? A technician looks for normal functions of the type described earlier. Then the machine is inspected for signs of forced entry. Chip seals are observed to insure that they are unbroken. EPROM chips are unsealed and tested to verify that the correct program was running. The whole process can take a couple of hours depending on the machine. Some casinos use this opportunity to run a background check on the player (to confirm that he/she doesn't have a history of defrauding casinos). In some jurisdictions a state inspector must also scrutinize the win. For

Smarter Bet Factoid
Wide-area progressives (progressive games linked across multiple properties) are typically owned by a slot manufacturer. The manufacturer leases the machines to the casinos, shares in the revenue, and is responsible for paying the top prize.

example, Mississippi gaming officials review all jackpots above $100,000.

If your jackpot makes it through this gauntlet, then the prize is yours. Time to celebrate!

WHEN THE SKY FALLS

What should you do if your jackpot is disputed? First, you should set aside any notion that the casino, the state, or the machine manufacturer is trying to "steal" the money by not paying you. Progressive jackpots are held in special accounts and are legally considered players' money waiting to be won. Regular jackpots come off the casino's bottom line, but they're a standard cost of doing business. Jackpots make great press. Everyone loves them. Everyone wants to pay, but they also want to follow the rules and avoid running afoul of the law. Remember Dolores Banyai? Imagine the hands that were spanked at the Hilton over that one.

Okay, you're thinking clearly. Now what? Consider the win. Was it clean? People have gone to court and litigated for years over symbols that almost lined up, machines that didn't lock up, and lights that didn't flash (or did). In most of these cases the RNG indicated no win or the machine had some other malfunction. Results of litigation have been mixed. Here are a few examples:

• Cengiz "Gene" Sengel thought he had won $1.8 million at Silver Legacy in Reno in 1996 when the reels stopped on a winning combination. But an inspection determined that the RNG didn't deliver a win. The bill receptacle in his machine malfunctioned; that froze the reels. Sengel went to court. Four years later Nevada's Supreme Court ruled against him.

• Sylvia Gutierrez thought she hit a $112,600 jackpot on a Betty Boop Thrillions machine in 1999 at the Sands Regency in Reno. The reels certainly said so. Bally disagreed. The machine did not lock up. There were no lights, bells, or an RNG win. One year later Bally caved in and cut a check. They had lost in court and decided not to appeal.

• Herminia Rodriquez nailed a $330,000 winning combination in 1997 as Harrah's Ak-Chin Casino in Arizona. The machine apparently malfunctioned, but Rodriquez didn't see it that way. She went to the media: a 64 year-old grandmother vs. the casino. Harrah's quickly paid up to end the bad publicity.

• Effie Freeman allegedly lined up the symbols for a $1.7 million win at Splash Casino in Tunica in 1995. Casino Data Systems said it was a hopper jam. The machine did not lock up. Four years later the Mississippi Supreme Court ruled against Freeman.

And the list goes on and on. Losers outnumber winners, but every case is unique.

For every dispute settled by a judge or jury there are thousands more that are resolved by the casino or regulators before reaching the courts.

And of course, some situations are clearly not wins. One obvious example is the catastrophe that occurs when a player smacks the top combination with less than a max bet. That's a $3,750 mistake when playing $1 video poker, and it can mean millions on a progressive. There's no legal maneuvering that can change that ugly reality. You must wager maximum credits to receive the top prize.

Will That Be Cash or Check?

When the gambling gods smile and the RNG concurs, then you have some important choices to make. Cash is a reasonable option if the win is under $2,000, but anything substantially over that is probably best taken as a check. Remember, hundreds and maybe thousands of people just saw you jumping up and down screaming, "I'm rich! I'm rich!" Bells were ringing and lights were flashing. It was hard to miss. A few of the spectators might have been crooks, so a wad of cash will make you a walking target. Request a check or put the money on hold at the casino's **cage** (the bank-like area where money transactions are conducted). Many casinos also offer direct deposit to a checking account. If you must carry cash then request a casino security escort to the car. Don't be shy about asking. That's their job.

But hey, you're not going to the car. That's because the casino is offering you a free room, meals, and by the way, could you sign this promotional release? They want to use your name and image for publicity. Some folks think it's a kick. Others prefer to remain anonymous. Do you want crazy Uncle Elmer to know that you're suddenly wealthy? It's a personal decision. Choose wisely.

EVERYBODY LOVES A WINNER

Smaller cash jackpots will be delivered as Ben Franklins with a few Andy Jacksons sprinkled on top. Do you suppose someone was expecting a tip?

A casino isn't a restaurant, so don't feel obliged to give away a big chunk. Some people tip the extra twenties. Others give one percent of the win ($100 for $10,000). One school of thought says that tipping is absurd if the jackpot doesn't negate losses for the trip.

On the other hand, remember that you're tipping for service. How long did you wait for payment? How were you treated? Did the casino staff make the win a happy experience, or did it seem like a

Smarter Bet Tip
Are you wondering what the current jackpot is on Megabucks or Quartermania? You can call toll-free and get the latest totals on those and all the wide-area progressives made by IGT. The number is (888)448-2WIN.

chore and a bother? Was it like Mardi Gras or a trip to the DMV? It's certainly appropriate to reward those who helped the process along, but you should definitely not tip if you waited a long time, more that thirty minutes for a standard jackpot. Wide-area progressives should take two to three hours, occasionally longer.

KEEP THE GOOD TIMES GOING

While you're waiting some "new friends" may appear and keep you company. They'll be very entertaining and they'll like you very much. You'll be invited to dinner, drinks, or maybe a party. Scrutinize these agreeable new companions carefully. Not everyone is a con artist, but don't let a giddy glow muddle your judgment. It's really a drag to win $4,000, foolishly take cash, go out with a new friend, and find the money and the friend missing when the bill comes.

We'll talk more about safety in Chapter 9.

Remember, a certain amount of winning is inevitable when you play regularly, but some losing is inevitable, too. Gambling lore is filled with stories of people who hit big and blew it all. Plan ahead, and you won't be one of them. Consult a financial advisor if the win is substantial then. Buy something that generates income. Don't plow everything back into the machines (unless you're purchasing gambling stocks). The glow lasts a lot longer when the cash stays in your pocket.

In Review

🍒 **Slot machine jackpots** of $1,200 or more in the U.S. are reported by the casino to the IRS. The form used for this is a W2G. Withholding is mandatory for amounts above $5,000 or for any amount when the player doesn't provide identification.

🍒 **Casinos in most states** require that a player provide identification before they pay a large jackpot. The most accepted form of identification is a state- or province-issued driver's license or identification card.

🍒 **Underage gamblers** are not paid jackpots. There are no exceptions to this rule

🍒 **The person who pushes the button** is the jackpot winner. Keep this in mind if you're playing one machine with another person.

🍒 **A regular jackpot** should be paid within thirty minutes. Wide-area progressives often take two or three hours before a check is cut.

🍒 **Always play maximum credits** if you want to be eligible for the top prize.

Chapter 6

Comps: Squeezing the System

MOST PLAYERS FIT ON A SPECTRUM BETWEEN THE FOLLOWING EXTREMES:

Hit-and-run: This person likes to play at many different casinos. It's Bellagio in the morning, Bally's in the afternoon, and Caesars at night.

Long-haul: Bettors of this variety sit down at a table or machine in one casino and don't move for hours.

Casinos prefer long-haul customers because they tend to lose more; they won't stop during a losing streak, and they stay at one venue. All casino financial and marketing systems are designed to encourage these players (who are described in the industry as being **casino-oriented**). Long-haul customers get the **comps** (complimentary rooms, meals, and other incentives). Hit-and-run players get a friendly smile and the bill for dinner. Red-carpet treatment is offered only when a player demonstrates that he or she is casino-oriented. All customers, including high rollers, are held to this standard. Comps are not an enticement. They are a compensation for allowing the casino a shot at your money.

Should you pursue this relationship? It depends. First let's explore how the comp system works, and then we'll examine its potential value for you.

Join the Club

Every major casino has a card system that electronically tracks and rates wagers. Getting into the rating system is really easy. You go to the players club desk, fill out a form, and the casino gives you a personalized card (it takes about a minute). Insert your card into the slot machine every time you play and the action will be recorded. Points accrue for dollars wagered. The casino offers comps and cash back for points. It also offers promotions and discounts for simply being a players club member.

Of course this is a casino, so everything isn't always entirely straightforward. The first mystery is how many dollars equal a point. Some club brochures clearly tell you. Some have fuzzy information, so you have to ask to find out. Occasionally you'll find clubs that treat the question as if you were requesting to audit their books.

Got a players club
question? Ask a
casino host (one of
the well-dressed
perpetually sociable
people you'll find
hanging around the
players club desk).
That person will
tell you how much
action is required
for a buffet, free
room, show ticket
or whatever other
comps the casino
is offering. It never
hurts to ask.

The second mystery is what you can get for the points. Most clubs have printed brochures that state clearly how many points it takes to get a comp room or comp meal, but they usually don't mention that a casino host, pit boss, or slots supervisor has the option to give you more. Another thing to consider is that video poker frequently earns points at half the rate of slots because video poker has a lower house edge.

THEORETICAL WIN AND FREE STUFF

Whatever you get and however the casino calculates points, the total value of comps is always based on a casino's **theoretical win**; that's the average amount the casino expects to earn from you. The actual net win or loss is usually not considered because every casino anticipates fluctuations (as you should). You may be lucky and another person may be unlucky, but variations inevitably become smaller over time as the totals get bigger.

In any case, a casino will typically comp about twenty to thirty percent of

Theoretical Casino Win and Typical Comps

House Edge	$0.50 Bets	$0.50 Comps	$1 Bets	$1 Comps	$5 Bets	$5 Comps
10%	$100.00	$25.00	$200.00	$50.00	$1,000.00	$250.00
9%	$90.00	$22.50	$180.00	$45.00	$900.00	$225.00
8%	$80.00	$20.00	$160.00	$40.00	$800.00	$200.00
7%	$70.00	$17.70	$140.00	$35.00	$700.00	$175.00
6%	$60.00	$15.00	$120.00	$30.00	$600.00	$150.00
5%	$50.00	$12.50	$100.00	$25.00	$500.00	$125.00
4%	$40.00	$10.00	$80.00	$20.00	$400.00	$100.00
3%	$30.00	$7.50	$60.00	$15.00	$300.00	$75.00
2%	$20.00	–	$40.00	–	$200.00	–
1%	$10.00	–	$20.00	–	$100.00	–

These figures are calculated on 500 decisions per hour, a four-hour day, and 25% comps. Machine payback is the inverse of house edge (92% payback = 8% house edge). Actual casino comps will vary by property.

the theoretical win. The table above shows you how it works. House edge is the inverse of machine payback (92 percent payback = 8 percent house edge). Keep in mind that these amounts are average. Some comp programs are more liberal than others.

Also, ten levels are provided here as an example, but most comp programs don't have so many levels. They usually have one tier for slots and another for video poker.

The first thing you'll notice is that a fifty-cent player on 92 percent payback slots will barely qualify for a free buffet (valued somewhere between $10 and $20) during a typical four-hour day. On the other hand, playing five-dollar bets on a 92 percent dollar machine for four hours is theoretically worth $800 to the casino and will probably get you about $200 back in comps. That's usually good for free **RFB** (room, food, and beverages) at a modest level. Also note that casinos generally assume everyone is losing at least three percent, so anyone playing with a near-zero edge usually gets comped at a higher level.

Now some people might ask, "Very interesting, but so what? The players club computer will track my play, and a casino host will simply tell me what I am entitled to receive. Right?"

Yes, or maybe no. There's no rule that says a host has to give you the maximum goodies allowed. Asking will sometimes get you something more. And wouldn't it be nice to know in advance how much your business is actually worth? How do you compare the players club at casino A vs. casino B when they have entirely different point systems? The best way to do it is with theoretical win.

Another advantage of these calculations is that they help you to see how much supposedly free comps actually cost. It's not bad luck that empties your pockets. Rather, it's average luck over time.

But all of the above advantages pale in comparison to the major reason why you should be gleefully sharpening your pencil to figure theoretical win. It's all about…

DOUBLE-DIPPING FOR FREEBIES

What would happen if you received comps for playing a 95 percent game, but you were actually playing a 99.5 percent game? Let's say you were wagering $5 per hand. You would "theoretically" lose $500 per day, but you would actually lose only $50 (on average). The casino would comp you $125, and that would put you ahead by $75 in real value.

Read the preceding paragraph again. Yes, it might seem too good to be true, but it happens every day for anyone who is willing to make an effort to play optimal strategy on a video poker machine.

Smarter Bet Factoid
Comps and the action required to get them can vary widely. Upper-tier properties like the big fancy palaces on the Las Vegas Strip generally require considerably more action for comped rooms and meals than smaller and older casinos.

As I explained in Chapter 2, most people don't use optimal strategy. So they lose. The casino is counting on it.

Isn't that wild?

We'll talk about video poker in the next few chapters, but for now let's wrap up comps.

Comp Caveats

You can see how the entire subject of comps gets players into a mindset of asking, "What do I have to do to earn comps? How much should I bet?"

Don't surrender to that mindset. Remember that comps are designed to keep you playing. Most people *lose* three to four times more than they receive, so the best way to handle comps is to not chase them. Join the players club at your favorite casinos, play as you would normally, and negotiate your comps separately.

Yes, there are some situations when the net value of comps will exceed your losses, and you might even be lucky and win at the machines, too. But there's no guarantee that any particular casino will have the right combination of loose machines and a liberal comp policy. Hard-core slot enthusiasts (mostly video poker players) diligently calculate the numbers and simply refuse to play when the conditions aren't right. They go somewhere else. You may not want to be so zealous. That's okay. Remember, you're playing for entertainment. Whatever you do, make sure you're having fun.

In Review

🍒 **Comps can be a valuable premium** that in some situations may offset your gaming expenses, but you should never play for comps. Join the players club at your favorite casinos, play as you would normally, and negotiate your comps separately.

🍒 **A casino's theoretical win** is an estimate of what the house expects to earn from you over a particular period of time. Comps are calculated on the basis of theoretical win. Twenty to thirty percent of the win will usually be comped back.

🍒 **There's no rule that says** a casino host has to give you the maximum goodies allowed. Asking will sometimes get you something more.

🍒 **It's always a good idea** to establish a relationship with a casino host if you intend to play a lot at one casino.

Part 3

Strategies for Video Poker

Chapter 7

Hunting the 100 Percent Payback Game

VIDEO POKER EXERTS A NEAR-MYSTICAL PULL ON MANY PLAYERS. It's the legendary frontier game combined with the best elements of a slot machine. That is powerful stuff.

The game also has some practical advantages compared to regular slots. There is no hidden house edge; no secretly tight machines. Each draw is from a freshly shuffled deck. Every hand requires a choice. It's a brainpower contest that pays. Video poker is one of the few casino games that has a positive expectation. That's right. Play the right machine, long enough, in the right way, and video poker is mathematically guaranteed to pay back more than it takes in.

But that doesn't mean you should quit your job to go play video poker. The effort required to earn a steady income as a gambler is a full-time job itself. On the other hand, it's fairly easy to play a near-neutral game (pushing the edge to just above or below zero). Add the value of comps, and video poker can be a ticket to a free or nearly free vacation.

Before we get into that (especially if you're skipping around in this book), please be sure to read Chapters 1, 2, 5, and 6 because the information there is the foundation for the strategies presented here.

Basic Video Poker

If you know poker then the fundamentals of video poker will be familiar. There is a hierarchy of hand ranks (see the next section) and a draw, but beyond that you should forget everything you know about the table game when playing the video version. You can't bluff the machine, raise, or call. There's no pot. The game deals you five cards. You can keep all of

Smarter Bet Tip

Some players become excited and forget to hold cards when they're dealt a royal flush or another perfect hand before the draw. One more press of the deal button does not bring a big payout, but five more cards. Ouch! Be sure to press the hold button for every card you intend to keep. The screen should acknowledge your choice.

them, some, or none. Replacements are dealt as necessary. The revised combination is your final hand. Winners are paid according to a pay table posted on the machine.

The most basic game is jacks or better; any hand with jacks or better is a winner. Other versions make deuces or jokers **wild** (they count as any value the player requires). Wild-card games typically raise the minimum winning hand to kings or better, two pairs, or three of a kind. Multiple-hand games allow you to repeat the same starting cards three, five, ten, fifty times, or more. Each time the draw is different.

Whatever the game, the play remains essentially the same; receive five cards, draw, the result is your hand (or hands).

Buttons on a video poker machine are similar to those on a slot machine except that "Spin" is replaced by "Deal," and each card has a button for holding. Newer video poker machines use touch screens and include computer-style help functions.

Ranking the Hands

Poker hands are ranked as follows:

ROYAL FLUSH: Ace, king, queen, jack, and ten of the same suit.

STRAIGHT FLUSH: Five cards of the same suit in exactly adjacent ranks.

FOUR OF A KIND: Four cards of the same rank and a fifth card of any rank and suit.

FULL HOUSE: Three cards of the same rank and a pair of another rank.

FLUSH: Five cards of the same suit that are not exactly adjacent ranks.

STRAIGHT: Five cards not of the same suit in exactly adjacent ranks. An ace can be used to make both the highest and the lowest straight.

THREE OF A KIND: Three cards of the same rank and two cards of different ranks.

TWO PAIRS: Two cards of one rank, two cards of another rank, and a fifth card of a third rank.

ONE PAIR: Two cards of one rank and three cards of different ranks.

NO PAIR: Five cards that don't make any combination.

The Pay Table IS the Game

The RNG in a typical slot machine is a mysterious mechanism. What's the payback? Who knows? It's all a big head-game. But video poker is different because the range of choices is fixed. The RNG simulates dealing from a shuffled deck of cards. No loose or tight machines. No mysterious house edge. No exceptions. Shuffle a deck at home and deal. The likelihood of receiving any particular hand from a real deck is identical to a video poker deck.

That makes the pay table the most important element of every video poker game. Here's why. A casino can't tighten or loosen a machine by changing how the cards are dealt, so the only way the house can get an edge is to change the payouts. Thus you can simply look at a pay table and (with a little practice) instantly know the casino's edge.

Consider the pay table for the venerable original version of video poker (see page 100). It's popularly called 9/6 because a full house pays nine and a flush pays six credits per credit wagered. This particular pay table returns 99.5 percent when the game is played with optimal strategy.

Some casinos think that 9/6 is too generous, so they reduce the payout for a full house to eight and a flush goes to five. Thus the game is called 8/5. That drops the overall payback to 97.3 percent. Lounges, convenience stores, and less competitive locations often have 6/5 machines. Those pay back only 95 percent.

Jacks or Better 9/6 Payable

Coins	1	2	3	4	5	Frequency	Return
Royal Flush	250	500	750	1000	4000	0.0025%	1.98%
Straight Flush	50	100	150	200	250	0.01%	0.55%
Four of a Kind	25	50	75	100	125	0.24%	5.9%
Full House	9	18	27	36	45	1.15%	10.3%
Flush	6	12	18	24	30	1.10%	6.6%
Straight	4	8	12	16	20	1.12%	4.5%
Three of a Kind	3	6	9	12	15	7.44%	22.3%
Two Pairs	2	4	6	8	10	12.9%	25.9%
Jacks or Better	1	2	3	4	5	21.46%	21.5%
Tens or Worse						54.54%	0%
Total						100%	99.5%

A typical pay table includes the unshaded area above. The figures in the shaded area are provided here to show you what happens when the game is played with optimal strategy. Note that each coin increases payments proportionally except for the fifth coin. That last extra credit quadruples the payment for a royal flush. Percentages are rounded.

Experienced players have learned to avoid the lower-paying machines, so casinos jigger pay tables in other ways to attract customers (see "Comparison of Pay Tables" on page 102). A typical ploy is to offer a bonus for four of a kind, and then to reduce the payout somewhere else on the table where the player doesn't notice. Double Bonus (B) looks like a 9/6 machine, but it's not. The payout for two pairs is only one coin.

Another gimmick is to make deuces or jokers wild, and then entirely delete the payment for a high pair or two pairs. Whoops! And then there are copycat versions. Look closely at the two columns on the far right of the chart. They're nearly identical except for the payout for four of a kind. The one-coin difference drops the return by nearly six percent.

There are dozens of different video poker versions, each with its own pay table, and each pay table requires a unique strategy. Yikes! Wait, don't go flipping back to the slots section. Video poker optimal strategy is easy to follow when you avoid machines with stingy pay tables, and learn to play just a few games that pay near 100 percent. I'll show you how to do that in the next chapter.

For now just remember that VP optimal strategy is all about finding good pay tables. Video poker pros typically won't play anything worse than 99.5 percent payback, but I recommend 97 percent as a low limit for casual players. In other words, stay away from 7/5 and 6/5 J-O-B. Scrutinize bonus games carefully (using the chart on the next page) to be sure all the hands are full-pay.

Comparison of Pay Tables

	JOB 9/6	JOB 8/5	Bonus Poker (LV)	Bonus Poker (AC)	Double Bonus (A)	Double Bonus (B)	Deuces Wild (full)	Deuces Wild (low)
Royal Flush	800	800	800	800	800	800	800	800
Four Deuces	-	-	-	-	-	-	200	200
Wild Royal	-	-	-	-	-	-	25	25
Five of a Kind	-	-	-	-	-	-	15	15
Straight Flush	50	50	50	100	50	50	9	9
Four Aces	-	-	80	50	160	160	-	-
Four 2s, 3s, 4s	-	-	40	40	80	80	-	-
Four of a Kind	25	25	25	20	50	50	5	4
Full House	9	8	8	8	10	9	3	3
Flush	6	5	5	5	7	6	2	2
Straight	4	4	4	4	5	5	2	2
Three of a Kind	3	3	3	3	3	3	1	1
Two Pairs	2	2	2	2	1	1	-	-
Jacks or Better	1	1	1	1	1	1	-	-
Payback	99.5%	97.3%	99.2%	98.3%	100.1%	97.8%	100.6%	94.3%

Payments and percentages are calculated per single unit wagered, but they reflect the bonus that is paid for max coins. Example: Royal flush is 4,000/5 = 800.

In Review

🍒 **Video poker uses standard poker-hand ranks** to determine winners. The most basic game is jacks or better. Deuces or jokers are wild in other versions. Wild-card games typically raise the minimum winning hand to kings or better, two pairs, or three of kind. Whatever the game, the play remains the same; receive five cards, discard and draw, the result is your hand.

🍒 **The RNG in a video poker machine** simulates dealing from a shuffled deck of cards. The likelihood of receiving any particular hand from a real deck is identical to a video poker deck.

🍒 **The pay table is the most important element** of a video poker game. A casino can't tighten or loosen a video poker game by changing how the cards are dealt, so the only way the house can get an edge is to change the pay table. Thus you can simply look at a machine and instantly know the casino's edge.

🍒 **Some machines pay slightly fewer coins** on selected hands. The difference may seem small, but it can dramatically increase the house edge.

Chapter 8

You Gotta Know When to Hold 'Em

GET READY, I'M GOING TO CROSS YOUR EYES IN THE NEXT PARAGRAPH. But don't worry, this is only an example.

Did you know that a double-inside three-card straight flush has a different expected value if it has no high cards vs. one high card? And did you know that those hands are different from a single-inside three-card straight flush with zero, one, or two high cards? They're all worth less than a sequential three-card straight flush with one high card. And of course, that affects the draw strategy if a five-card combination includes one of the above and two high cards of another suit.

You probably didn't know that, and I don't blame you. Video poker purists revel in these subtle nuances that increase the return by fractions of a percent, but I'm guessing that you'd like the game to be a bit easier. So strictly speaking, the strategies in this chapter are less than optimal. They're very close but intentionally *not* perfect because twenty lines is easier to memorize than thirty-six lines. A shorter strategy generally sacrifices a portion of a percent for the sake of convenience, but simply using the strategy (rather than guessing) will improve your overall game by five percent or more.

Jacks or Better

The following strategy works for "plain vanilla" (no bonus) jacks-or-better games with 9/6 and 8/5 pay tables. You can also use it on 7/5, 6/5, 10/6, 9/7, and most bonus contests that pay 1-2-3-4 at the bottom end of the table. Examples of these games can be found in the chart on page 102.

The way to use the strategy is to match your hand to the highest one in the list and then play as directed. So if your hand is 2♦ 7♦ 8♦ J♦ J♥, you hold the two jacks instead of the four-card flush or three-card straight flush because a high pair is highest on the list.

Here are some more examples:

10♥ 8♦ J♠ 10♠ 9♠ This hand should be played as a low pair (hold the tens) rather than as a four-card straight, two-card royal, or three-card straight flush.

Jacks or Better Strategy

Hand	Discard
Royal or straight flush	0
Four of a kind	1
Four-card royal	1
Full house, flush, or straight	0
Three of a kind	2
Four-card straight flush (open-ended or with a gap)	1
Two pairs	1
High pair (jacks or better)	3
Three-card royal	2
Four-card flush	1
Low pair (tens or lower)	3
Four-card straight (open-ended)	1
Two-card royal (two suited cards jack or higher)	3
Three-card straight flush (open-ended or with gaps)	2
Ace, king, queen, and jack unsuited	1
King, queen, and jack unsuited	2
Two high cards (drop an ace if necessary)	3
Suited high card and ten	3
One high card (jack or higher)	4
Toss everything	5

The above strategy works for "plain vanilla" no-bonus jacks-or-better games that pay 9/6, 8/5, 7/5, 6/5, 10/6, and 9/7. This strategy also can be used with most bonus games that pay 1-2-3-4 at the bottom end of the table.

A♥ K♦ Q♥ J♥ 10♥ Yes, you should bust a perfectly good straight for the chance of hitting a royal flush. Discard the king.

3♦ 3♣ Q♠ 6♥ 9♥ Hold the low pair. Resist the temptation to also hold the queen. Keeping extra high cards (known as **kickers**) dramatically reduces the chance of improving to quads, trips, two pairs, and such.

7♣ 8♣ 10♥ J♥ A♠ Hold the two high cards. By the way, you should never draw to an inside straight (a straight requiring one rank) except A-K-Q-J. Outside straights can be made with two ranks, so an outside draw is twice as likely to succeed.

2♥ 9♠ A♥ Q♣ J♦ Hold the queen and jack. Do *not* hold an unsuited ace with two other unsuited high cards. Of course, if the ace in this example were diamonds, you would keep the two-card royal and drop the unsuited queen.

Deuces Wild

Deuces wild strategy is radically different from jacks or better. One pair, two pairs, and worse (97 percent of all starting hands) are worthless without a deuce or a good draw. Of course, the wild cards make paying hands easier to construct, but those hands aren't worth as much, so the game tends to be more volatile even though it often has a greater long-term return. The "full pay" version of deuces wild (see page 102) is more than one percent better than 9/6 J-O-B, but you may not notice it unless you stick around for the royals.

Deuces Wild Strategy

Hand		Discard
Hands With Four Deuces	Four Deuces	1
Hands With Three Deuces	Royal flush	0
	Five of a kind	0
	Three deuces	2
Hands With Two Deuces	Royal flush	0
	Five of a kind	0
	Straight flush	0
	Four of a kind	1
	Four-card royal	1
	Four-card straight flush (open-ended)	1
	Two deuces	3
Hands With One Deuce	Royal flush	0
	Five of a kind	0
	Straight flush	0
	Four of a kind	1
	Four-card royal	1
	Full House	0
	Four-card straight flush (open-ended)	1
	Flush or straight	0
	Three of a kind	2
	Three-card royal	2

Deuces Wild Strategy

	Hand	Discard
	Three-card straight flush (open-ended)	2
	One deuce	4
Hands With No Deuces	Royal flush	0
	Four-card royal	1
	Straight flush	0
	Four of a kind	1
	Full house, flush, or straight	0
	Three of a kind	2
	Four-card straight flush (open-ended or gapped)	1
	Three-card royal	2
	Pair	3
	Four-card flush	1
	Four-card straight (open-ended or gapped)	1
	Three-card straight flush (open-ended or gapped)	1
	Two-card royal	3
	Toss everything	5

The above strategy works for full-pay deuces wild and most other versions. Note that a pat straight flush is *not* held when it's made with three deuces, and a pat full house, flush, and straight, are not held when they're made with two deuces.

The strategy on the preceding pages works on full-pay deuces wild, and it also works reasonably well on most other versions, notably the popular and generally available almost-full-pay 800/200/25/16/10/4/4/3/2/1 that returns over 99 percent.

Here's a closer look at the strategy:

J♥ J♣ 4♦ 4♣ 6♠ Two pairs are worthless, so drop one of the pairs (it doesn't matter which one) and the extra card.

2♦ 2♥ J♠ 9♣ A♥ Don't be tempted by the three-card royal or the four-card straight. Keep the two deuces and discard the rest.

A♦ 2♦ J♠ 10♠ 4♠ Yes, a four-card flush is staring you in the face, but it's not very valuable when made with one deuce (which is why it's not on the list). Go for the three-card royal.

K♣ J♥ 8♠ A♠ 3♦ It looks promising, and then you realize this is deuces wild. Toss all five cards.

7♦ Q♥ 2♦ K♥ Q♦ Hold the queens and deuce (making three of a kind). That ranks higher than the three-card royal.

Optimal Strategies in Action

Take another look at the J-O-B pay table in Chapter 7. You'll notice that the royal flush is worth roughly two percent of the payback, but that includes the bonus for maximum coins. If you play less than the maximum, you're giving up a tremendous edge. Unlike slots optimal strategy, there is no circumstance in which single coins are favorable. Always bet the max per hand. If that's too expensive, drop down to a lower denomination.

Once you've chosen a denomination, the next step is finding a favorable pay table. You'll be tempted to play machines based on their outward appearance, but take your time and stroll through the casino. Beginners often see a confusing swirl of numbers, so it might help to carry a slip of paper with four or five pay tables written on it. Then you can compare the machines to known payouts. You can also write down unfamiliar pay tables and study them later.

As with slots optimal strategy, you should begin a session with at least 150 times your per-hand standard bet. Remember that a "hand" in this situation isn't necessarily a lone five-card combination because you might be playing multiple five-card hands simultaneously.

VOLATILITY COMPARISONS

Jacks or better games come in three primary types. The traditional games (9/6, 8/5, and such) change the payouts only on the lines for full house and flush. Bonus games change those two lines and also offer a bonus for quads. Double-bonus games do all that and they also typically lower the payout on two pairs from two coins to one.

Deuces wild games entirely drop the bottom payouts, and they push the wins even further up into the higher hands.

Video poker optimal strategy does not change when multiple hands are played simultaneously. One hand should be played the same way as four, ten, or fifty hands. However, the overall volatility goes down with multiple hands because losers are combined with winners. That makes jackpots smaller, but it reduces the possibility of a bet returning nothing.

As you know, bigger jackpots toward the top mean less is available in the middle or bottom. Thus jacks or better is the least volatile video poker version. Bonus poker is more volatile, and double bonus and deuces wild are the most volatile.

Why would people want to play volatile games? They do it for excitement. You can expect to see quads about once an hour when playing jacks or better. That's $125 on a 9/6 one-dollar machine, but bonus or double-bonus games will pay $200, $400, $800, or even more in some circumstances (depending on the rank of the cards). You can look forward to one or two of those in a typical half-day session. Oh yeah!

Of course, those mini-jackpots don't affect the long term payback, but some people enjoy the extra short-term action.

By the way, volatility is the reason why I don't recommend using standard J-O-B strategy on double bonus games. The full strategy for double bonus is about fifty lines, and you'll need it to get the most out of that contest. On the other hand, the sky won't fall if you play a double bonus game with standard J-O-B strategy (it's better than slots). But don't blow your bankroll.

Also, I didn't include a strategy for joker poker in this book, partly because of its volatility and mostly because there are too few full-pay versions out there and too many copycat low-paying versions. See the resources section in Chapter 9 for joker poker and double bonus strategies.

HERE WE GO!

Choose your game and settle in. Machine-hopping is entirely unnecessary once you've found the right pay table. There is no such thing as a "tight" video poker machine. There is only good luck and bad luck. Of course, I always encourage people to wander and poke around just for fun. Move if it pleases you. You may find an even better pay table across the aisle, but staying put is perfectly okay when playing video poker.

Another thing that's perfectly okay is carrying your strategy on a small card or slip of paper (or taking this book with you). There's no rule that says you have to play only from memory. Even pros occasionally get stumped. The more you practice, the more you'll remember, and pretty soon you'll be zooming through the hands.

While you're zooming, keep in mind that optimal strategy identifies the combination with the greatest long-term expected value, but it doesn't guarantee that any particular draw will be successful.

Look at the chart on page 100. More than half of J-O-B hands are losers. About 21 percent return the original wager, and only about 24 percent actually return a profit. In other words, you're going to lose sometimes even when you play a perfect strategy.

PROGRESSIVES: THE VIDEO POKER PERSPECTIVE

Remember how I told you to stay away from progressives in the slots section? Well, all that changes when you're playing video poker. Progressives are a good thing when they reach a certain value (this takes a bit of calculating, but it's definitely worth the effort). Here's an example.

A 4,000-coin royal flush is worth about 2 percent of total payback. Right? That's $1,000 on a single-hand quarter machine. Let's say you're looking at an 8/5 quarter machine with a $3,000 progressive jackpot. You know an 8/5 typically returns 97.3 percent, and that *includes* the normal value of a royal. But the progressive royal is three times larger (2% + 2% + 2%) That is four percent more payback than normal. Add 97.3 and 4; the total is over 101 percent. Should you play this game? Absolutely! It's a positive-expectation contest.

But wait a second! What if you don't hit the royal today, tomorrow, or whenever? What if someone else hits the top prize? That may happen, but it's okay because your gambling life is one long session. Ditto for the casino's gambling life. Just make good bets every day, and the long-run will take care of itself.

In Review

 Always bet maximum credits when playing video poker. If that's too expensive, drop down to a lower denomination.

 Traditional jacks or better (no bonus) is the least volatile video poker version. Bonus poker is more volatile, and double bonus and deuces wild are the most volatile.

 Machine-hopping is entirely unnecessary once you've found the right pay table. There is no such thing as a "tight" video poker machine.

 It's a good idea to carry a slip of paper with pay tables and a strategy when you go to the casino (or bring this book). That will help you find the best games and play them correctly.

Chapter 9

Safety, Taxes, and More

"HEY, YOU DROPPED SOME COINS."

That's how the scam starts. The player sees a well-dressed man or woman pointing to the floor beneath the seat. The scammer smiles and the player bends over to retrieve the money. When she comes back up her purse or coin cup is gone. So is the crook.

It's unfortunate, but the mixture of money, confusing noises, tourists in "fun mode," and the constant push of the crowd in a casino creates a prime environment for larceny. Purses, wallets, bags, cups of coins, chips, and anything not nailed down or attached to one's body are in danger of disappearing into a mass of pulsing humanity.

Here are some tips to help you avoid becoming a statistic:

• Don't carry a purse or bag. If you must bring a bag, place it securely between your legs or in your lap when sitting.

• Thieves often use a loud noise or a nearby disturbance to distract attention while they grab unattended items. If you hear a loud noise or you see a disturbance, look down and secure your belongings before you look up to see what is happening.

• If someone bumps into you hard enough to knock you off balance, don't worry about who will apologize to whom. Immediately assume you are being robbed. Hold tightly onto anything you want to keep because in the next millisecond it will be forcibly torn from your hand, arm, or pocket. Also, beware when you're "accidentally" doused with a spilled drink. The loud ditzy blonde who is frenetically dabbing your gin-soaked crotch may be covering for a confederate who is scooping up your chips.

The Little Things That Count

Always remember to cash out and remove your players club card when leaving a machine. Yes, it sounds crazy but people forget to do that. Conversely, be sure to put your players club card into the machine before playing. And here are some other things to remember:

• A casino advertisement may claim that certain slots or slot areas "pay up to 98 percent," but this doesn't necessarily mean that all the machines are loose. A few games may be loose, and the rest may be very tight.

- Video poker machines that are advertised as "certified to pay back more than 100 percent" will only do so if you play maximum coins and use optimal strategy.
- It never hurts to ask a casino employee where the loose slots are, but it rarely helps. Strategy will help you more than hot tips.
- Always play maximum coins on a progressive game.
- Stick to your limits. Stop when your session bankroll is spent. Exit a machine when you reach your stop-loss or win-limit. Don't give in to superstition or temptation. Follow your strategy.

SLOT TOURNAMENTS

Tournaments are a good way to get a lot of playing time for not a lot of money, and you also have an increased probability of smacking a big prize (because the top contestants are guaranteed to win). Some tournaments are free or they have a low entry fee. Others are multiple-day affairs and cost hundred of dollars, but the expensive ones usually have big prizes and come with hotel rooms and other perks.

Here's how to calculate if the tournament entry fee is a good value. Add the prizes together and divide by the number of contestants. Then subtract that amount from the fee and you'll have the dollars per person held back by the casino (essentially the gross casino profit after prizes and before expenses). Compare that to the value of the room, meals, and other perks. Beware of tournaments where the pool of contestants can expand without an appropriate expansion of the prize structure.

All the machines in a tournament are identical (ultra-loose), so quick fingers and luck are all that matter when playing slots. It's mostly strategy when playing video poker, though luck and speed play a larger role than normal because the tournament has a time limit.

CRUISE SHIPS, SLOT JOINTS, AND THE INTERNET

There's nothing wrong with betting a few dollars in an unfamiliar place, but you should only play "serious" money at licensed casinos that report earnings to local regulators. That means cruise ships, most Internet casinos, and other loosely-regulated gambling venues (including some Native-American properties) are not necessarily where you'll get the best game. What if an RNG doesn't allow a royal flush? Oops! Guess you'll have to complain to the gambling commissioner in Belize.

Slots are enough of a gamble by themselves. You don't need the extra excitement of wondering if the games are rigged.

Smarter Bet Tip
It's easy to slip into a bad mood or be fatigued without realizing it, especially in the heat of a game. You should stop playing when you're tired. Stop when you're hungry. Stop when you're frustrated. Remember, games should be fun. If you're not having fun, go do something else.

GAMBLING AND TAXES

All your gambling income is taxable in the United States, even if a win doesn't reach the W2G threshold for mandatory reporting by the casino to the IRS. It's simple. You win money; you owe Uncle Sam.

Gambling losses are deductible, but only when they offset gambling profits. And you must keep detailed records of those losses or the IRS will disallow them if you are audited. You'll need to list exactly how much you lost on a particular day at a specific game. List the machine numbers.

Sure, it's a hassle, but remember that this is all about winning.

Resources

Here are a couple of Internet resources that you'll find helpful:

The Las Vegas Forum *http://go.compuserve.com/lasvegas* This is a comprehensive message board dedicated to the subjects of Las Vegas and gambling. It has thousands of items covering hundreds of subjects, and a large library set aside specifically for slots and video poker. The site is hosted by CompuServe, but it's free and available to everyone on the web.

SmarterBet.com *http://www.smarterbet.com* This site is dedicated to all of the Smarter Bet Guides. You'll find additional information here about slots, video poker full-length strategies, strategies for other gambling games, more Internet links, and an e-mail link so you can send me questions.

Now you've got all the tools to be a winner. Go for it!

In Review

🍒 **Keep an eye on your personal belongings** when you're in a casino. Avoid carrying a purse or bag. Use the casino cage when handling large amounts of cash, or ask for a security escort.

🍒 **Avoid alcohol when you're playing.** Stop playing when you're tired, hungry, or frustrated. Games should be fun. If you're not having fun, go do something else.

🍒 **Tournaments** are a good way to get a lot of playing time for not a lot of money. Most are free or reasonably priced, but beware of tournaments where the pool of contestants can expand without an appropriate expansion of the prize structure.

🍒 **Gambling losses are deductible,** but only when they offset gambling profits. And you must keep detailed records of those losses or the IRS will disallow them if you are audited.

🍒 **Don't wager too much** at loosely-regulated venues like Internet casinos and cruise ships.

Glossary

action Refers to the amount of money wagered in a game. More money is synonymous with more action.

banking game See progressive.

bankroll An amount of money set aside specifically for gambling.

bonus multiplier A game that adds a bonus to the top prize when a player wagers maximum coins.

buy-a-pay A game that allows a player to buy an opportunity to hit additional winning combinations. In other words, three bars are worth 50 coins and three sevens are worth nothing if you wager one dollar, but two dollars will "activate" the sevens, and they'll be worth 100 coins if they hit.

cage The bank-like area of the casino where money transactions are conducted.

casino host A casino employee who administers the players club.

casino-oriented A term used in the gaming industry to describe a customer who plays and who frequently strongly prefers one property. Casinos seek customers who are casino-oriented.

comps Complimentary rewards such as free meals, free rooms, free shows, and travel reimbursements. A casino give comps to players who are perceived to be casino-oriented.

draw A poker term commonly used in video poker. To "draw" is to throw away cards and receive replacements in the hopes of improving a hand.

flat top A slot machine with a top prize that is fixed, a non-progressive amount. See progressive.

gambler's fallacy Refers to the myth that past results affect the current contest.

hand-pay A jackpot that is paid by a casino employee.

house edge The financial advantage a casino has in a wager. House edge is usually expressed as a percentage.

house odds The amount a casino will pay for a winning bet. Not to be confused with true odds.

jackpot A slot machine prize.

kicker An unsuited card held in draw poker, usually as a bluff. Kickers should never be held in video poker.

multiplier A game that pays exact multiples of whatever amount is wagered.

negative expectation A wager or series of wagers with a long-term disadvantage (from a player's perspective). A game that retains more money in the long run than it pays.

nudge A game in which a winning symbol sometimes hits just above or below the payline, then clicks into position to create a paying combination.

once-through A bankroll stop-loss system that allows each dollar in a bankroll to be risked exactly once.

optimal strategy A system of play that lowers or eliminates the casino's advantage.

pay table The schedule posted on a slot machine that shows how much is paid for each winning combination.

payline The line on a slot machine where the symbols must appear to indicate a win. Some slot machines have multiple paylines.

payoff odds See house odds.

players club A comp system that uses a card to track wagers. The casino rewards players on a scale proportionate to their level of action.

positive expectation A wager or series of wagers with a long-term advantage (from a player's point of view). A game that pays more money in the long run than it retains.

progressive A slot machine jackpot that gradually increases in value every time the game is played.

push A tie, the player doesn't win or lose.

random number generator (RNG) The heart of a slot machine. An RNG is a computer chip that randomly generates numbers to determine the exact reel position or specific cards that appear during a slot game.

reel One of three or more wheels inside a slot machine that are visible through a window at the front of the device. Various winning symbols are printed on each reel.

reel-spinners Slot machine games that use physical reels (as opposed to video reels).

RFB A casino-industry abbreviation for "room, food, and beverages".

rolling stop-loss A combination of a stop-loss and a win-limit that prevents a player from risking winnings beyond a particular dollar amount.

session A period of time designated for gambling.

stop A section of a slot machine's reel that is covered with a symbol, or in some cases intentionally left blank.

stop-loss A plan for exiting a game when a particular amount of money has been lost.

theoretical win The average amount the casino expects to earn from a customer. Theoretical win is calculated by multiplying the total action (total amount wagered) by the house edge.

toke Casino industry jargon for a tip (gratuity).

tower light A light on the top of a slot machine that indicates when the machine has malfunctioned or has registered a jackpot.

true odds The true probability of winning or losing a contest. Not to be confused with house odds.

win-limit A plan for exiting a game when a particular win goal has been reached.

Index

Numbers followed by *f* and *t* indicate figures and tables.

Acknowledgments

Thanks to Ron Luks, Randy Ripley, Dave Wink, and Dane Addison for their comments and suggestions. Thanks to Fay Nestor for her loving support.

Special thanks and kudos to my editor Sharyn Rosart. Her vision and determination have made the Smarter Bet series possible. Thanks also to Lynne Yeamans for her design.

About the Author

Basil Nestor is an author, journalist, columnist for *Casino Player* magazine, and creator of *CompuServe's* advice series *Ask the Gambling Expert*.

He has worked with CBS, NBC, CNN, PBS, and other television networks as an editor and producer. Basil created the award-winning documentary *Casinos in the Community*, an in-depth look at the gaming industry in Atlantic City. He also produced *Riverboat*, a television documentary that reveals how gaming is changing the Midwest. Basil has authored six books (including *The Unofficial Guide to Casino Gambling*) and dozens of articles for *Casino Player* and other magazines. Basil is also a frequent contributor to *CompuServe's Las Vegas Forum*.

Got a gambling question? Visit *SmarterBet.com* and send Basil an e-mail.